PRAISE FOR *RAISING MEN, NOT BOYS*

Christians understand that God created human beings as male and female—for His glory and for our good. The differences between the sexes are not matters of evolutionary accident, but are clear indications of God's sublime and perfect design for human happiness. Yet in our age, confusing cultural signals have led many boys and young men to be uncertain and unaware of their masculinity and proper role in the home and in society. This brave new book by Mike Fabarez is a faithful guide for parents who want to raise their young boys to become true men. Full of Scripture-informed wisdom, this is a message parents and young boys need to hear. May God make us faithful as we seek to lead our boys to become true Christian men.

R. ALBERT MOHLER JR.
President of the Southern Baptist Theological Seminary

Raising Men, Not Boys is an absolutely brilliant look at specifics relevant to boys of all ages and the most complete book about raising boys I've read. If your son is an infant, read it now. If he is older, read it now. Read sections out loud to him so he understands himself and why you're making the decisions you are. Underline sections, fold over page corners, and remember to come back to it again and again as your boys experience more of life. Moms should absolutely read this. Differences between boys and girls are very real! Dads should read it, too, of course. Your sons will become men motivated to live for God and equipped to glorify Him if you read, believe, and put into practice just the truths from chapter 2. Mike Fabarez's explanation of the elements of the gospel and what's relevant for spiritual growth and wellness is the best I've read. This chapter is worth the entire price of the book. Read it all, though. You'll be glad you did.

KATHY KOCH
Founder/president of Celebrate Kids, Inc.
Author of *8 Great Smarts* and *Screens and Teens*

In this marvelous handbook, veteran pastor and experienced father Mike Fabarez provides a deeply probing discussion of various areas every Christian parent of sons should consider in their raising of those boys to become the men God wants them to be. Pastor Fabarez has thought through this subject carefully and includes so many valuable, crucial, and insightful reflections on areas responsible Christian parents would be wise to implement. Let me put it simply: Raising sons? Get this book! You'll be so grateful that you did.

BRUCE A. WARE
Professor of Christian Theology, The Southern Baptist Theological Seminary; author of *Big Truths for Young Hearts*

You can tell a lot about a man by the children he raises. Fabarez's sons tell a definitive story about an intentional father. Turning boys into men doesn't happen by accident. This character comes about by the shepherding of a devoted father. Others now have the chance to learn from him in *Raising Men, Not Boys*. Read this volume and join the ranks of intentional fathers.

DAN DUMAS
Overseer of the State of Kentucky's Adoption and Foster Care System
Coauthor of *A Guide to Biblical Manhood*

As a father trying to shepherd my son into a man, I am thankful for this helpful resource from Mike Fabarez. He tackles hard issues with balance and precision while continually casting a vision for what godly parenting looks like. Every parent of boys needs to read this book.

THOMAS WHITE
President of Cedarville University

We'd never consider building a house without a set of blueprints. Yet every day many of us are building families without a blueprint—a vision of what we're working towards. This book is your blueprint for raising the next generation of men. Read it, soak in the truth, and lead your son intentionally.

JILL SAVAGE
Author of *No More Perfect Kids* and *No More Perfect Marriages*

No doubt you've heard the stories of teen boys who skip class to play video games, or live with mom and dad as adults. Why aren't more boys maturing successfully into men? This book will help you raise your son intentionally and biblically, with hope and a game plan.

ARLENE PELLICANE
Speaker and author of *Parents Rising* and *Growing Up Social*

Boys will be boys, but at some point they must be turned into men, godly men. In this book, Mike Fabarez provides a toolbox of biblical principles and patterns that will help today's parent to shape a generation of young men who embrace their masculinity, God-given calling, and need to follow the man Christ Jesus. Read this book, and I pray that God will use it to help you raise a Peter not a Peter Pan.

PHILIP DE COURCY
Pastor of Kindred Community Church
Teacher on the daily radio program Know the Truth

Raising sons to be strong, godly men is hard work. Mike Fabarez explains why this work is essential and how to do it well to the glory of God. Fathers, read this book!

H. B. CHARLES JR.
Shiloh Metropolitan Baptist Church

RAISING MEN, NOT BOYS

SHEPHERDING YOUR SONS TO BE MEN OF GOD

MIKE FABAREZ

MOODY PUBLISHERS

CHICAGO

Edited by Jim Vincent
Interior design: Ragont Design
Cover design: Evangela BeSharpCreative LLC
Author photo: Luke Melrose

Library of Congress Cataloging-in-Publication Data

Names: Fabarez, Michael, 1964- author.
Title: Raising men, not boys : shepherding your sons to be men of God / Mike
  Fabarez.
Description: Chicago, IL : Moody Publishers, [2017] | Includes
  bibliographical references.
Identifiers: LCCN 2017021250 (print) | LCCN 2017032219 (ebook) | ISBN
  9780802495679 | ISBN 9780802416575
Subjects: LCSH: Parents--Religious life. | Parent and child--Religious
  aspects--Christianity. | Parenting--Religious aspects--Christianity. |
  Child rearing--Religious aspects--Christianity. | Men (Christian theology)
  | Boys--Religious life.
Classification: LCC BV4529 (ebook) | LCC BV4529 .F24 2017 (print) | DDC
  248.8/45--dc23
LC record available at https://lccn.loc.gov/2017021250

We hope you enjoy this book from Moody Publishers. Our goal is to provide high-quality, thought-provoking books and products that connect truth to your real needs and challenges. For more information on other books and products written and produced from a biblical perspective, go to www.moodypublishers.com or write to:

Moody Publishers
820 N. LaSalle Boulevard
Chicago, IL 60610

1 3 5 7 9 10 8 6 4 2

Printed in the United States of America

CONTENTS

But What About . . .

ANSWERS TO CHALLENGING QUESTIONS

FOREWORD

Raising kids in this day and age—what a challenge! Raising boys to be courageous, godly men who will lead well and hold to the kind of values and perspective about life that are desperately needed in our world today can seem like a daunting and overwhelming task.

Having experienced first-hand the destruction and pain a lack of loving, consistent parenting and fatherly leadership can wreak in a young boy's life, I am grateful to be able to say that investing in and thoughtfully parenting the next generation can make all the difference in the world. Applying the truths found in God's Word to the task of parenting will bring us the hope and encouragement we need to avoid the pitfalls inherent in the child-rearing philosophies and values of our fallen sinful world.

In *Raising Men, Not Boys*, Mike Fabarez not only addresses important foundational principles and goals for raising boys to grow up to be self-controlled, respectable young men, but also provides practical advice to help parents think through how they might accomplish these ends. We are encouraged to ask the right questions and set priorities by envisioning our boys' futures as men. We discover how routine disciplines and practical routines, like making sure our young boys "sweat" every day, sleep enough, complete their homework and chores, as well as learning how to handle money, love, serve others, and rightly value and interface with the women God puts in their lives, will prepare them to make the biggest possible impact for Christ.

Pastor Mike uses illustrations and examples from his own life experience of raising two boys who are now young men. You will be revived and challenged not to throw in the towel, but to diligently prepare your young sons to face the world. No, there are no guarantees, but we as Christians are called to faithfully apply the principles and priorities found in God's Word to the task of parenting, as we prayerfully work to raise men, not boys.

Josh McDowell
Author of *10 Commitments for Dads* and
Straight Talk with Your Kids about Sex

Introduction

A WHOLE
NEW BALLGAME

It seems like yesterday when I was fumbling with the straps of
the newly purchased car seat, trying to situate our newborn baby boy
into the idling car in the loading zone of our local hospital. Two days
earlier my wife, Carlynn, had struggled through some seemingly endless thirty-three hours of labor to bring our firstborn into the world.

We had waited and prayed ten years for this child. After countless
months of disappointment and all the cyclical pain of infertility, God
had finally blessed us with the first of what would be two little Fabarez
boys—who we were tempted to believe would never be.

Our motionless, little Matthew was all strapped in and we were
on our short three-mile drive home. I found myself driving more
cautiously than I had for my driving exam on my sixteenth birthday,
making full, deliberate stops at all the stop signs, and triple-checking
my blind spots with every lane change. In a few minutes, we pulled up
to our little condo.

My wife was understandably exhausted. As she waddled into the
house I valiantly carried little Matthew into the living room. Unsure

as to where to put him, I chose to lay him face up on the sofa. Carlynn settled into a chair, while I slowly stepped back from our sleeping seven-pound baby and took a mental picture that I am sure I will never forget. The house was silent, my wife's eyes were closing, one of little Matthew's arms was stretched out by his side while the other curled along the side of his head. I broke the silence with a soft-spoken, yet very sincere question: "What now?"

Everything had changed. Sure, we had read books and taken notes as we observed our friends raise their kids, but bringing one of our own home was a whole new ballgame. We were committed to doing things right. We wanted to please God as parents, and as a pastor of a growing church, I had already preached more than one series of sermons on key passages in the Bible about raising children. But now it was our turn.

Our two boys are grown now, out of the house, and off to college. Matthew's brother, John, came just eighteen months after his big brother, and compounded the energy and testosterone in our home over the years. We learned something of how unique these man-children were when God blessed our family with their little sister, Stephanie. It has been a joy and a challenge to seek to raise up two men for the glory of God. It is my hope that this book might be used to help you as you seek to do the same.

THE MODERN CHALLENGE

Raising up men for the glory of God will likely be far more difficult for our generation than it has been for several generations past. Consider the moral confusion that surrounds any discussion of gender these days—particularly when we are talking about men. With the definition of gender itself being called into question at every level of society, it is no wonder that identifying the goals of parenting a male child seem daunting. When our culture can't even agree on what it is to be a man, we will need a great deal of courage to stand on the divinely delivered definitions found in God's Word.

The modern social commentators have gone so far as to try to persuade our generation that there is "no one type of body that we could accurately label a 'male body.'"[1] Not only are our children supposed to self-identify as to gender in any of a number of ways as they might choose, but now we are being told that it is wrong to even suggest that one has been born with a male body, because it is as they say "a choice to refer to some bodies as male and some bodies as female, not a fact."[2] If we are to believe the cultural elite, we can no longer label our baby boys and girls by their gender, and we dare not raise them according to some outdated set of definitions of masculinity and femininity, even if we took our cues from the objectivity of biology.

But of course, our definitions of boy and girl, man and woman, are not outdated; they are eternal. Biology has meaning, and its meaning is explained to us by our Creator. The world's attempts at redefining our children and lecturing us about a person's whims and wants being preeminent over God's design will prove in the end to be futile. Yes, it will take courage to operate by God's truth as parents, but there is no real option for those of us who know the true and living God. Christ is Lord. For us there is no other way. For all their efforts to shame us for being on the "wrong side of history," the true follower of Christ recognizes that those who live their lives in submission to God's revealed truth are in fact the only ones who will actually be on the *right* side of history.

THE RULE-MAKER

The world may have opinions, but those who understand the reality of the Creator God who has revealed Himself know there is only one lawgiver (Isa. 33:22; James 4:12). Because God exists and has clearly revealed His will regarding male and female, parenting and godliness, there is only one voice that really matters amid all the noise of our society's ideas. And while present society may want to label all definitive statements contrary to their opinion polls as hateful and intolerant, the most loving thing we Christians can do is to plainly confess, reiterate, and live out God's spelled-out designs and instructions.

Actually, God's directions have always been called into question and held suspect, not because they are inferior or "don't work," but because a spiritual battle has been waging from the time God gave the first command to the first family. Recall how Satan was quick to whisper, "Did God actually say . . . ?" when it came to the Lord's plan "A" for human beings (Gen. 3:1). If you are just beginning to raise a family, or you have adolescent boys bounding with energy and opinions, remember the truth of Scripture about them (and us): there is and will always be a "spirit that is now at work in the sons of disobedience," one that flows in the present "course of this world" (Eph. 2:2–3). In other words, we ought to expect the world to be pushing a contrary and rebellious plan for just about everything that is truly good, right, and profitable. Satan is the father of lies, Jesus told us (John 8:44), and he seems to be working overtime, spewing his deceptive and destructive alternatives to God's clearly established plans for raising boys and training them to become men.

GOD'S TRUSTWORTHY INSTRUCTIONS

Without apology, throughout this book I will continually draw your attention to the timeless truth of God's Word. I would hope that those who pick up a book for Christian parents would already be sold on this concept, but in our day, that may not always be a safe assumption. So at least let me briefly state that the Bible is not man's best thoughts about God, but rather—and there is ample evidence—the Bible is in fact God's thoughts on paper. Not only has the sustained impact and influence of the Bible been remarkable, but the fact that it contains a vast number of specific predictive prophetic statements which have come true shows us that this is a book men could not have crafted themselves. God is the only one who knows and can declare "the end from the beginning" (Isa. 46:9–10). He has punctuated His Book with so many exacting prophecies, the sort of which cannot be found in any other religious book, that we should be convinced that His signature is all over the Bible.

When God undoubtedly signs a document that is filled with practical definitions, instructions, and commands, we would be fools to assign the Bible a place with every other "authority." God has spoken, and His Word should hold an exclusive and preeminent place in our quest to understand what is right, good, and true. So, let us unashamedly look to God's Word as we seek to raise our children and guide our boys in becoming the men God has designed them to be.

THE MAN-RAISING COMMUNITY

While the African proverb "It takes a village to raise a child" has been largely hijacked by the feminist and socialist voices of our generation, the acknowledgement primarily applies to parents: we need more than what's found within the four walls of our home to raise our kids. As mothers and fathers we need to quickly confess that truth. Our kids, especially our boys, need to be nurtured and fostered by a larger community of shared values. That, of course, is what the church is to provide us as Christians.

Active involvement in a local church is an essential component in seeing our boys become godly men. It is arrogant, or at best short-sighted, to think that the role models and Christian discipleship our boys need are only found in their relationships with Mom and Dad. I am so thankful that from their youngest years my boys have been incorporated and engaged with the Christians in our church. It is a kind of fostering of their lives, which is just not possible within their immediate and even extended family. The iron that sharpens iron (see Prov. 27:17) can be employed by God in your church. If you don't have a church home, or your standards have been so impossibly high that you haven't plugged in, it's time for that to change. You need church. Your boys need church. Find one that is committed to the teaching of God's Word and draw near to that church community. Get involved, and know that the formation of your boys will depend in part on a community of Christians with whom they connect, serve, and worship. Many of the principles laid out in this book will focus on the home and your direct involvement as a parent, but remember that everything discussed will be against the backdrop of your larger participation in your local church.

"SPIRITUAL COMMON SENSE" (NOT MANDATED TECHNIQUES)

Over the years of preaching, counseling, and holding question-and-answer sessions on the topic of parenting, I have collected the most valuable content of what I have come to call the "spiritual common sense" of raising our boys. This describes a kind of teaching of the principles of God's Word that extends to the *practicals* of how these timeless truths are implemented in our daily decisions about our kids. The following chapters will seek to drive these principles to that place. Not because this is the way all Christians should do it, but because sometimes the suggested wisdom for the real-life scenarios we face as parents can become an instructive and helpful kind of biblical advice.

Having seen the abuses of many of the formulaic and technique-driven methods of parenting, I am careful to avoid the "this-is-the-only-godly-way" of applying the biblical principles. But I will try to flesh out suggested applications that we have found to be profitable. Even so, I will attempt to include an adequate number of disclaimers to remind you from time to time that there is a difference between the *certain* application of God's Word, and a *possible* application of God's Word.

For example, if one were to consider the exhortation from the apostle Paul to young Timothy, the pastor of the church at Ephesus, found in 2 Timothy 2:15 (i.e., "Do your best to present yourself to God as one approved, . . . rightly handling the word of truth"), one could with absolutely biblical authority demand that young pastors give a high priority to the study of God's Word. On the other hand, while it may not come with divine authority, a wise counselor with years of experience in studying and preaching God's Word might provide the "spiritual common sense" that to effectively prove to be an unashamed student of the Scriptures, one should not leave the study of God's Word and the preparation of a sermon to the night before one has to preach. The former exhortation is a certain application of God's Word, while the latter, though not carrying the full weight of biblical authority, is a possible application and would certainly prove to be a profitable and helpful directive to young pastors.

It is my hope that the mix of *certain* and *possible* applications of biblical principles related to the raising of young men presented in this book will prove to be advantageous in your work of bringing up your sons.

ENVISION A MAN'S
FUTURE EVERY DAY

I am told that in Seattle, Washington, a very progressive and trend-setting slice of our Western culture, keeping dogs as pets now outnumbers raising children by a rate of four to one. As demographer Jonathan Last reports in his cleverly named book, *What to Expect When No One's Expecting,* the modern dog-ownership preference has so impacted cities in America and Asia that schools are rapidly being replaced by doggie daycare centers and playgrounds with dog parks. At the same time, money lavishly spent by couples on their dogs is overshadowing our parents' monetary investment in us.[1]

The problem with our culture's exploding doggie-ownership trend is that those who still choose to brave having human children will often subconsciously adopt a "children as pets" mentality. That may sound crass, but think about it—deciding to have a child is often entered into as some kind of life-enhancing, joy-producing, satisfaction-inducing endeavor. Without ever verbalizing their motives, couples often pursue having children because they believe "a baby will make us *happy,*" "children will *complete* us," or simply just because "we've always *wanted* kids."

Sure, raising children will at times bring parents joy and gratification, but when our reasons for having a baby are indistinguishable from the reasons we might pick out a puppy at the animal shelter, we have entirely missed God's intentions for the propagation of the human race.

THE PLAN AND BLESSING FOR CHILDREN

The very first couple received a foundational calling in the familiar words "Be fruitful and multiply" (Gen. 1:28), and repeated various times.[2] With the laudable (and rare) exception of forsaking marriage and family for the sake of kingdom advancement, in the spirit of Jesus Christ Himself (Matt. 19:12), raising children to produce the next generational society is to be the norm. Unless you are a confirmed "kingdom single," the biblical expectation is the covenant of marriage and the subsequent engagement in raising children for the fulfillment of God's global plan and for Christ's eternal glory.

The big perspective then is that your little boy was not entrusted to you to bring you joy, fulfill you, or make you happy—though I pray he will. His temporary consignment to your family is to prepare him to take his place in this world as a trophy of God's grace and as an agent of God's values and priorities in this upcoming generation.

The Scriptures tell us children are the glory of their parents (Prov. 17:6). A simple yet profound readjustment of our parenting mindset makes analogies like the one found in Psalm 127 come to life. God illustrates the role of a mom and dad like this: "Behold, children are a heritage from the LORD, the fruit of the womb a reward. Like arrows in the hand of a warrior are the children of one's youth. Blessed is the man who fills his quiver with them!" (Ps. 127:3–5a).

It is considered a blessing in God's economy to be a spiritual archer in your generation, having a case over your shoulder filled with young children that you are aiming and launching into the next generation! What a vivid *and rare* perspective on being a parent. Your boy is for a time in your home, under your care, and in proximity of your influence to be thoughtfully pointed, and launched, and propelled into the future to make a strategic impact for the Lord's good purposes.

Can you see how this perspective can transform your perspective from the very beginning? So many modern parents' voices begin to quiver when they imagine their little boy growing up. They lament the thought of him one day moving out and moving on. They see his forthcoming maturity as some kind of foreboding eventuality, instead of as the whole point of having him in the first place: the gratifying goal of shooting these arrows into the world that God has planned for them to impact.

So, from the beginning get this truth in your heart and mind. That squirmy little infant you bring home from the hospital is, in a short number of years, intended by God's design to step into His world as a young man who will make a difference for Christ. Your job is to release him to this reality. Your goal cannot be to "hang on to him as long as possible." Your hope must be to see him become that independent, mature, functioning adult. God has made this arrangement very clear.

LEAVING, CLEAVING, AND LEAVING

After describing the first marriage officiated by God in the garden of Eden, Moses added an inspired commentary that is applicable to us all—telling us that the marriage relationship is to be permanent, while the parenting relationship is to be temporary. Yes, you and your wife will always be his parents, and he can benefit from your advice—if he asks for it. But once he marries, your parenting responsibilities have ended.

By God's design, parents are in effect heading toward a "divorce" of sorts from their children, while they are to remain bonded together in their marriages until "death do us part." Our society has this completely backwards!

Read these foundational words afresh: "Therefore a man shall leave his father and his mother and hold fast to his wife, and they shall become one flesh" (Gen. 2:24).

These are strong words in the original Hebrew language, both for separating from our parents and for being joined to our marriage partner. It could hardly be stated more emphatically. Marriage is a bonding together of a man and a woman with such a profound relational adhesion that, Christ stated, what God has joined together, man should not separate (Matt. 19:6). Then, just as we adults were directed in this divine design to make a clean and comprehensive separation from our childhood dependence and reliance on our parents as we stepped into adulthood and marriage, so our children will do the same when they come of age. Each of us left the temporary arrangement of our childhood homes to cleave together in what is to be a permanent bond, and we are then to anticipate and expect that our children will do the same.

How often our fallen world has turned this upside down, as parents try to explain their divorce to the kids, saying, "While Mommy and Daddy will no longer be married, you, Johnny, will always be *my little boy*." It may be so common these days that it sounds like the right thing to say when a marriage "falls apart."

But consider the truth of what should be impressed upon our sons, something to the effect of "Your mom will always be my wife, and you will no longer be my little boy, but will be a man with his own wife and family." When my wife and I revealed that this had been the common sentiment expressed to our sons from their youngest years, many of our friends were aghast, thinking we were kidding. And when they realized we weren't, they suspected that such talk must have bred some sort of insecurity in our boys. Nothing could be further from the truth. Our boys, like all other boys, flourished with the sense of security of knowing that their mom and dad are committed to one another through thick and thin. They will also thrive, mature, and grow when they know that mom and dad's expectation is for them to grow into independent and productive leaders in the church, in society, and in their own families.

GOD'S DESIGN FOR GROWN MEN

The image of an independent and productive leader does not need to be manufactured from our imagination, or from some character sketch out of a movie or novel. God has provided a picture of what men are to be in the very first chapter of the Bible. Consider the words of Genesis 1, which give us a peek into God's design for who He created us to be.

> Then God said, "Let us make man in our image, after our like-ness. And let them have dominion over the fish of the sea and over the birds of the heavens and over the livestock and over all the earth and over every creeping thing that creeps on the earth." So God created man in his own image, in the image of God he created him; male and female he created them. And God blessed them. And God said to them, "Be fruitful and mul-tiply and fill the earth and subdue it, and have dominion over the fish of the sea and over the birds of the heavens and over every living thing that moves on the earth." (Gen. 1:26–28)

This foundational statement describes what Adam and all of his subsequent sons were purposed to be—and who our boys are soon to become. God gets to lay down the expectation for His creatures. He is the Boss. And while there are many competing voices telling us what a successful son should look like, the Maker gets to make that determination.

It reminds me of the din of competing voices we heard when our boys played Little League baseball. A rambunctious crowd was always shouting at my sons to swing for the fences, while a dugout full of team-mates also had opinions as to what they might want my boys to do at the plate. Of course, there was Mom, who was often most concerned with their safety and welfare.

The crowd may want my boys to take a huge cut at the ball, their teammates may shout their various opinions, and Mom may just want them to be careful, but it is the coach who gets to direct their time at bat. He may call for a sacrifice fly, a bunt, or a hit and run. He is the coach. My son's future on the team, his commendation or criticism, will depend on his response to one singular voice. How wise we would be to realize the same, as we aim our sons into their future. One day our boys will stand as men to answer before their Creator. I trust they will be able to testify that their mom and dad set them on a course which sought to fulfill their ultimate and most fundamental calling as men.

Here are four noble goals for our sons as men, each found in our key passage: to know God, exercise proper authority, and, if married, love their wives and replicate themselves.

1. Men Who Know God

When God created the first man, He made him unique from every other creature He had created. He determined to make man "in his own image" and "after his own likeness." This, of course, cannot possibly be referring to some kind of physical template. The Bible tells us that "God is spirit" in the essence of who He is (John 4:24), and "a spirit does not have flesh and bones" (Luke 24:39). So when God created the first man, the "likeness" must refer to his nature and his capacity to relate to God. Just as the triune God has relational fellowship within the persons of the Godhead, so Adam was created as a person who could have relational fellowship with the persons of the Godhead.

The Lord made Adam to know Him and relate to Him in a way that no other part of the physical creation was capable of doing up until that point. Psalm 100:3 provides the needed perspective on why we were initially created: "Know that the LORD, he is God! It is he who made us, and we are his; we are his people." The Westminster Shorter

Catechism asks as its first question, "What is the chief end of man?" It answers: "Man's chief end is to glorify God, and to enjoy him forever." That enjoyment of knowing and having fellowship with our Maker is the most fundamental purpose for every man's existence.

Much more can and will be said on this important aspect of nurturing and developing our sons' interests and desires to know God, but at the outset let me simply remind parents that there is a big difference between knowing about God, and knowing God. Our boys may have much exposure to the facts about God and the gospel, but until they establish a real and vital relationship with their Maker, our prayers and our work are only preliminary.

Consider the two sons of an Old Testament priest named Eli. They surely knew much about God. They were serving in the worship center. They knew much about the Bible and were engaged in "ministry," yet the Bible says this about them: "The sons of Eli were worthless men. They did not know the LORD" (1 Sam. 2:12).

Much like the "good theology" of demons, who we are told intellectually affirm all sorts of undeniable truths about God, they are still "worthless" and condemned because their "belief" is simply a head knowledge and not a genuine trust that establishes and feeds a bona fide relationship (James 2:19). God is jealous for our boys to become men who truly know Him (James 4:4–5). As parents, this must be our ultimate goal for our sons.

Many parents who speak of their son's future say, "I just want him to be happy!" I pray we will never mindlessly recite that mantra of our generation; let us instead say, "If only my boy would know the Lord!" Nothing could be more central to his existence than this.

2. Men Who Exercise Dominion

In the very next phrase of Genesis 1:26 God tells us that Adam was created to "exercise dominion" over the created world. Of course, Adam only had access to a limited part of that world, but "dominion" over his small corner of the world was to be his calling. "Dominion": now there's a word with a regal flare to it. Let's make sure we have a sense of what it is that God is calling our sons to grow up to do.

The word "dominion" refers to the application of a positive and constructive oversight over aspects of God's creation for good purposes. It is the exercise of leadership that brings out the best in what is overseen. Like the word "jurisdiction," it speaks to the management and engagement of thoughtful supervision that makes rules and gives directions in hopes of positive and godly results. In light of the associated phrase, "subdue it," which God employs two verses later to further clarify this calling, the idea of "dominion" depicts an active involvement of cultivating and taming aspects of the world that will be better and more useful when this kind of leadership is exercised.

As I like to say, we men were created to "subdue" and "exercise dominion" over our little corner of the world, yet many of us fail to gain dominion even over our garages, at least initially. Still, at some point in our adult lives we will experience the gratifying feeling of "gaining control" over an unruly garage, after some purposeful determination. In almost every job that a man may have he is given a little corner of creation over which to exercise dominion. The questions are: Are we exercising dominion well—and regarding it as a part of the core calling that traces its way back to the garden of Eden? Are we at work to faithfully exercise dominion not only over work projects or job goals, but also over our desks, our lockers, and hallway closets?

I put it that way because when we turn to think of our sons, we need to realize that putting their toys away or cleaning their rooms is not just some childhood necessity to avoid chaos, but it really begins to help them realize an experience not unlike one of the central callings on their lives as men.

Your boy's little corner of the world, no matter how small (a toy box, a dresser drawer, a set of baseball cards), is something where he enters into an exercise of leadership that God created him to experience. As parents we need to encourage these early steps of subduing the chaotic, and arranging and rearranging what can be improved and made more useful. We need to celebrate the good and constructive exercise of leadership wherever it might be found and envision where these positive and godly skills might be used to change his corner of the world for good.

3. Men Who Love Their Wives

When God created humanity to be a reflection of His intellectual, emotional, and volitional image, He didn't just create men; He created men and women. Recall the words of Genesis 1: "So God created man in his own image, in the image of God he created him; male and female he created them" (Gen. 1:27). In Adam's case He didn't just create a world that contained women, He purposed for him to participate in a marriage relationship with a specially crafted female counterpart named Eve. This complementary and special creation of God served to bring in the fullness of the reflection of His divine image in the human race. That is an important fact for all men to remember, whether or not they are ever called to participate in marriage.

From the earliest days, our little boys need to be taught that those little girls they innately perceive as cootie-infested irritants, are in fact a specially valued and divinely prized part of God's highest creation. The world is not what it ought to be and can never reflect the glory God intended without the women God created to display His own character. As old-fashioned as it may sound, boys need to grow into men who have the highest respect and courtesy toward the women in this world. Sin may have greatly complicated the relationship between men and women, but our boys must be trained to envision the grand and glorious plan of God in filling the earth with glory through the expression of male and female in their world.

Without ruling out the unique calling of becoming a "kingdom single," as I've called it, we must begin to instill the thoughtful expectation in our boys that they will one day be husbands. Much more will be said about this in chapters 3 and 8, but for now let us at least get comfortable envisioning and discussing the eventuality that our boys will one day be husbands, called to the daily tasks of providing, protecting, and sacrificially leading in their own marriages. Instead of avoiding

But What About . . .

STAYING SINGLE

Let's acknowledge that some sons may be among the few who "forsake marriage for the sake of the kingdom." Of course, Jesus never married, nor did the apostle Paul, and it's likely the devoted prophets Jeremiah and John the Baptist also remained single during their service to God.[3] They all were godly and fulfilled their purpose on this earth.

In modern times, some Christian men still remain single and are strong servants of the Lord, including preachers and theologians. Bestselling author John Stott noted that those who remain single "voluntarily put marriage aside, either temporarily or permanently," that they may "undertake some work for the kingdom which demands single-minded devotion."[4] The great twentieth-century Christian apologist and writer C. S. Lewis remained single until age fifty-six.

They are in that minority who have a God-given ability to find genuine contentment and peace with the absence of marital intimacy (1 Cor. 7:7). We can and should celebrate and applaud this special giftedness, but even if it is suspected that our son possesses it, we should not stop the conversations about his mentoring and discipling others.

these topics when our boys are young, let us be free to say things like, "When you are a husband . . . ," "When your wife is . . . ," and "When your marriage has. . . ." In a world where many males linger for decades in perpetual boyhood, punctuating our conversation with expectant and anticipatory discussions like this will go a long way in preparing our young men for their futures.

4. Men Who Replicate Themselves

Having already touched on the concept of being fruitful and multiplying (Gen. 1:28), for the sake of understanding our own role in raising adults-in-the-making, let us briefly consider this concept for our own children. Yes, some sons may be among those who are content to "forsake marriage for the sake of the kingdom" (Matt. 19:12). And some prophets and disciples possessed this giftedness (see "But What About"). Such blessed service for the King continues to this day. Yet this is the exception and not the general rule. Even if we suspect that our son has this special giftedness, we should not stop the conversations about discipling and coaching others. In a very important sense, there is no "kingdom single" presented to us in the Bible or throughout church history who did not replicate himself.

Most of our sons will find wives and be blessed to have children— and that is a reality they need to see from the beginning as a truly blessed reality. Most Christian parents can attest that the blessing of children goes far, fulfilling God's great design. For a mom and a dad there is something divinely satisfying in nurturing, sacrificing, and caring for their own children. Our little boys need to begin to sense this, not only by the way they perceive our enjoyment in parenting (which admittedly is not a nonstop joy ride, but should include enough smiles and laughter to be convincing), but also especially by the way we talk about the reality of their own future children.

My boys can confess that their childhood was punctuated by a number of comments that began with: "When you're a dad . . . ," "Be sure your kids get to . . . ," and "Don't ever let my grandkids. . . ." Often it was in a lighthearted moment, but many times it was not. It has been interesting to see how these periodic comments have produced serious questions from my boys about parenting, and how to handle this or that situation with their future kids. What a relief to know that my kids were not raised to see children as a burden or an obstacle to their "happiness," but as a genuine blessing from God.

AIMING AT INDEPENDENCE

Now before we get to the *practicals* and consider some "spiritual common sense" in seeking to live in light of what the Bible says our future men are to become, let's address one big problem. It is an obstacle that stands in the way of almost any attempt to foster independent young men: the problem of fear.

The Problem of Fear

Although many statistics on the harms to children are down across the board, stories about kids being harmed are clearly way up—compared to any previous generation. Our connected world in this information age, coupled with publishers and parents who want to "make us aware" of every conceivable threat to well-being, have us believe that it would be a miracle if our boys ever survive to adulthood. I am well aware that every statistic represents an incident of real harm, but we have to consider the millions upon millions of successful trips to the park, uneventful skateboard rides, and safe experiences in a boyhood activity that are never reported. The odds of a serious injury on just about every front are down, yet the fears of modern parents are through the roof.

It is time for every parent to revisit the words of Christ: "Are not two sparrows sold for a penny? And not one of them will fall to the ground apart from your Father. But even the hairs of your head are all numbered. Fear not, therefore; you are of more value than many sparrows" (Matt. 10:29–31).

It is true that sparrows sometimes fall to the ground, but Jesus was clear (as perplexing as His statement may appear), not a single one does so apart from the oversight and purview of God the Father. This is certainly not a license to be frivolous or careless (Luke 4:9–12), but it should remind us that overly cautious, worry-filled, helicopter parenting is useless. Again, in the words of Jesus, "And which of you by being anxious can add a single hour to his span of life?" (Matt. 6:27).

The righteous understand this and they are rightly fearless and free from anxiety (Prov. 28:1). Not reckless, but fearless. Not foolish, but assured that in a very real sense our sons are immortal until the day God has ordained as their last (Ps. 139:16).

Babysitters

One of the recurring chances for your children to learn independence is when Mom and Dad are away. This is also a chance for both the parents and their children to confront their fears. From the very beginning of our sons' lives there are many situations when Mom and Dad need time alone for a date night, a church service, ministry demands, or just a few hours to catch their breath. That's when the thought of "another" caregiver becomes an imaginative breeding ground for all sorts of "what ifs" for parents. *So many things could go wrong*, we would think. Even if your family caretaker is a grandparent, a trusted family friend, or the local church nursery, it's easy to imagine the terrible thing that just might happen if we are not there.

I remember once being out with my wife, having put my firstborn son in the care of his grandmother, only to get a phone call halfway through the night that my boy had knocked out his front teeth. Our first fanatical thought was that somehow had we been home he'd still have his front teeth. Well, not so. My mother-in-law wasn't throwing my kid around the family room like a football, or carelessly filing her nails in some backroom while my kid ran wild. No, my boy tripped on a step and slammed his mouth on the tile floor. I suppose a helmet would have prevented it, but the risk of toddling around the house *barefaced* is one most reasonable parents and grandparents take.

Those first experiences of separation from mom and dad are the very beginning of a future of increasing independence for your sons (and daughters). When *separation anxiety* kicks into high gear for you—and your toddler or young child whines—or even cries—as you walk out the door, remember that God is ultimately the one who keeps his heart beating and ultimately watches over him. These reasonable and needed hours apart (shorter times at first, perhaps longer later) are the initial experiences of him learning to manage without your moment-by-moment involvement. This is a small part of training your children for independence.

Bedtime, Clothing, and Chores

Here are three related activities that bring opportunities for your child to learn independence: bedtimes, clothing choices, and chores. *Bedtimes* and *nap times* are occasions to train your little boy to have the *big boy* experience of managing himself in the solitude of his bed. I know there is plenty of material written to the contrary—much of which is readily accepted by parents whose apron strings prove to be steel cables. But without debating the "experts," I can say from the laboratory of life, my wife and I have found that insisting our little boys stay in their beds and only call if there was a serious problem (like a gashed forehead) proved to develop young boys who could manage their own restlessness and get themselves to sleep.

I can say that because of our early investment in training our boys to independently get themselves to sleep, my wife and I cannot recall a single instance of them getting out of their beds and venturing downstairs to find us, or knocking on our bedroom door, or climbing in our bed at night. Sure, there was the periodic call for this problem or that scare, after which we lovingly invested a few minutes to address the problem. But our investment in teaching them to manage themselves during their naps and bedtime developed a boyhood skill that made everyone's lives much more peaceful.

Often parents give their young children far too many choices. But there are many situations where a parent can provide options, and in some cases even autonomy. Through such opportunities our growing boys can learn to be leaders of their own lives and to practice good decision-making. One is *clothing choices*.

Carlynn and I often let our preschool-aged boys pick their clothes to wear. Of course, parents always hold veto power over their boy's clothing choices, but when my boy is just hanging out on a Saturday, I certainly want him to learn to make decisions for his day, which can begin with what to wear. It may be a favorite jersey or T-shirt with a cartoon character on it. Learning to pick out his clothes is a good and generally safe "exercise of dominion" over his little corner of the world.

Even as my boys grew older, I was willing for them to make some relatively bad decisions, like deciding to leave the jacket behind or wearing flip-flops instead of tennis shoes (always with a clear warning as to what I thought the best decision would be); these decisions allowed them to regret their poor choices an hour or two later. Even in something as simple as being a little uncomfortable for an hour or two, failing to heed my counsel on bringing a jacket does wonders in instilling wisdom about the good and bad judgment that can be employed in making independent choices.

Doing chores helps boys learn responsibility and independence. My boys have always been assigned chores, but as they entered their teenage years, Carlynn and I were always looking for ways to encourage them to take on greater responsibility for their own lives. Giving them autonomy (within reason) over a set of chores, like doing all of their own laundry, helped to instill a sense of responsibility and "dominion" over a number of things that have a direct impact on their lives.

How helpful it is for young men to learn that clothes don't magically clean themselves. How good for them to begin to learn the independence of managing the washer and dryer, which otherwise would be a rude awakening by their second week away at college. No matter the age of your boys, continue to look for age-appropriate duties and responsibilities that have a direct impact on their comfort and daily convenience. And don't always insist things be done exactly the way you would do them; let them learn through their own trial and error that folded clothes and shirts hung on hangers, for instance, usually wear better than those that aren't.

INDEPENDENCE AND PLAYING OUTSIDE

Most people born before 1970 had freedom to play and ride most places, as long as they told parents where they were going and when they'd be back. We would leave the house on a Saturday morning and not have to be home until the street lights came on. We'd ride our bikes for miles and play in three different parks on one day, all without satellite trackers and smartphones. Today, anything similar to that might be grounds for calling Child Protective Services on the "absentee" parents. While I am not making a case that a previous generation of parents did everything right, there is something to be said about how many of us learned to manage situations, solve problems, and become increasingly independent by the freedom granted to us in our childhood playtime.

With the many incidents of child abduction and abuse, it is likely impossible to ever return to the childhood freedoms of yesteryear. Still, we need to give our boys some space to play, explore, and even get injured from time to time. Good parenting in the home means that our boys can venture outside the home without parents biting their fingernails, or keeping them on an incredibly tight leash. Yes, there ought to be wise boundaries and parameters, but all too often I hear of parents who view their own backyard as a dangerous and scary place their boys have no business exploring. Unless our boys have opportunity to exercise some reasonable area of dominion in their playtime, it is hard to imagine they will ever learn the necessary courage and determination to do much of any import in the tumultuous world in which we live.

ABOUT FORMS AND APPLICATIONS

Unlike ancient times, much of our modern world consists of forms, contracts, applications, and red tape. It was my goal to introduce my sons to this challenging aspect of modern life as early as they were able to do something to meet it. If there was a form to fill out at the doctor's office and they were old enough to write legibly, I would direct them to fill it in as I coached them. When they were old enough to enroll for driver's education, I would assign them to do the research on the computer, find three or four viable options, and bring their findings to me for input. When it was time for college, I would assign deadlines and quotas for the various applications, essays, and correspondence, providing them the accountability to ensure they got it all done.

If something needs to be done for our kids, and there is red tape involved, enlist your boys to be a part of the process. It is inconceivable that they will enter any kind of profession in this world which will *not* necessitate them being able to work through electronic applications, forms, and the paperwork of modern life. Get them to feel proficient at this whenever an appropriate opportunity arises.

APPLAUSE, PLEASE

It should go without saying, but let me say it anyway. Knowing that we are seeking to launch competent and productive men into the next generation, any time you see your young man show an aptitude at making a good decision, standing on his own, or being the "big boy" who can manage a situation on his own, applaud him with appropriate praise and affirmation. Let him know that these skills will serve him well, as God places him in the world to do something important for Him. Tell him that the good management he applied to a situation was an act that brings glory to God and will prepare him for adult life.

You can even salvage an unwise choice as a learning opportunity. Being decisive and taking a risk can be a good thing, even if the result doesn't prove to be advantageous. We don't want our boys paralyzed to make decisions because they are so fearful of making bad decisions. A productive adult life will surely call for a countless number of decisions, and not all of them will be the best ones. Praise him for learning that lesson even when his choices could have been better.

Encourage him in these small steps because you see their importance, having learned to prayerfully envision his future every day.

SET HIS SPIRITUAL TRAJECTORY

Jesus asked a simple and completely logical question, the point of which is so often missed by today's parents. It is a question that every person, and in our case, every Christian parent, must take some time to seriously ponder. Jesus asked, "What does it profit a man to gain the whole world and forfeit his soul?" (Mark 8:36).

Imagine for a moment that your little boy grows up to become one of the richest, most successful, most influential men of his generation—books are written about him, and high schools are named after him. Wow! That would certainly make any parent proud. But wait a minute, Jesus is telling His listeners. How will any man benefit, if after all that worldly success, he dies, stands before his Creator, and hears these dreadful words: "I never knew you, depart from me . . . Depart from me, you cursed, into the eternal fire prepared for the devil and his angels" (Matt. 7:23; 25:41)?

Your pride as a parent would certainly be short-lived. What real profit, joy, or happiness would there be on behalf of one who is eternally lost? How glad could one be for a man who never secured a prosperous afterlife? What lasting gratification can be derived from a son's fame and fortune, earthly pleasure and temporal happiness, if it is all to end with him having to bear the enduring penalty for all of his sins?

Jesus is obviously making a supremely important point that every parent should ponder. There is no real profit in earthly profits, if a person's soul is never redeemed and forgiven. This is an unsettling concern, which should motivate every Christian parent.

EVERY MAN'S NEED

It must be kept in mind that no matter how cute and adorable a newborn boy might be, he enters our world with a serious and far-reaching problem. Contrary to what many assume, human beings are not born into the world as blank slates or morally neutral beings. We are all "conceived in sin" (Ps. 51:5), as descendants of fallen ancestors (Gen. 3:20), sharing the same sinful nature as the rest of fallen humanity (Rom. 5:12–21).

The residual effects of our first parents' rebellion against God are present in every child. Consider the biological effects of sin's impact on our infants in something as common as a viral infection, or as serious as a life-threatening and debilitating birth defect, as was the case in the birth of my daughter. Every person's vulnerability to the power of death, regardless of age, is convincing evidence that all humans share in the wages of Adam's disobedience.

Thinking beyond the physical consequences of humanity's fundamental problem, consider the far more serious manifestations, namely the propensity to continue the pattern of sin and rebellion against God's righteous laws. Our boys don't enter the world with a bent to do what is righteous (as charming as they may at times be to their mothers and grandmothers); they are predisposed to do what the Bible defines as sin. They fall short of God's glorious standards and exist as young fallen humans, relationally alienated from the life of God. In other words, our boys need to be reconciled to their Maker, they need to be redeemed by Christ's death on their behalf, and they need to be declared righteous by the regenerating work of the Holy Spirit.

This life-changing conversion of sinners should be the ardent hope and prayer of every Christian parent. We should want more than anything for our sons to come to a place of rightly understanding their need for the gospel of Jesus Christ. We ought to be praying that they will experience a profound sense of conviction over their own sins, and see the incomparable value of Christ's suffering on their behalf. None of this is possible without the work of God's Spirit in their lives. I trust we can say with the apostle Paul, "My heart's desire and prayer to God for them is that they may be saved" (Rom. 10:1).

OUR GOD PRIORITY

Yes, we should all start with prayer for their salvation, but what else should parents do in hope and preparation for their son's expression of genuine repentance and saving faith? The knowledge and awareness of God ought to permeate our homes. Moms and dads need to speak of the importance and presence of God in all that we do. Our discussions of history, the daily news, and forecasts of where our world is headed should always find their way back to who God is, what He has revealed, and how He is actively involved in all things. In short, the existence and activity of God is the lens through which a godly Christian home must view and discuss the world in everyday conversations.

This is called a worldview. Everyone has one, and those who are going to raise up young men with a spiritual priority and a serious investment in God's kingdom must have a thoroughly Christian worldview.

This simple reminder can be convicting for us as parents. It may reveal our own need to think more biblically. It might expose a lack in our own spiritual maturity. Jesus said, "A disciple is not above his teacher, but everyone when he is fully trained will be like his teacher" (Luke 6:40). It is sobering to consider that as a general rule the spiritual sensitivities and investments we hope for our children will rarely surpass our own.

I suppose this is why so many are motivated to step up their own spiritual disciplines and pursuit of God when they have kids. So be it. It is a good time for us as parents to consider our spiritual health and resolve to be all that God desires us to be as His sons or daughters. We wouldn't want to send our boys to a batting coach who hits .200 or a golf coach who rarely breaks 100. So too, we ought to feel the pressure as our sons' primary Christian coaches, and make certain we are making gains in learning to "love the Lord our God with all our heart and with all our soul and with all our mind" (Matt. 22:37).

What I am getting at is that if we are hoping to "train up a child in the way he should go" so that "even when he is old he will not depart from it" (Prov. 22:6), he is going to need to see this God priority modeled. And as is often the case, learning to value and prioritize the things of God as a young boy is not only taught, but it is also caught. Here are three big areas.

1. A Bible-Saturated Home

If your sons are to become acquainted with the true and living God (and not some "god" of your or their imagination), then your household discussions about God need to consist of the truths about God that have been revealed in His written word, the Scriptures. As some of the first parenting instructions God gave reveal, "These words that I command you today shall be on your heart. You shall teach them diligently to your children, and shall talk of them when you sit in your house, and when you walk by the way, and when you lie down, and when you rise" (Deut. 6:6–7).

Scriptural words and biblical principles ought to saturate your home. Your conversation needs to regularly find its way back to the truth found in the Bible. Again, this is not likely to happen if Mom and Dad are neglecting their daily time in the Word. Be diligent about making time for your own personal Bible study. Guard it as an essential investment of your mornings (or evenings). Then be sure to leave that personal time with something from the Word; whenever possible share and discuss with your children. As J. C. Ryle rightly said:

> You cannot make your children love the Bible, I allow. None but the Holy Ghost can give us a heart to delight in the Word. But you can make your children acquainted with the Bible; and be sure they cannot be acquainted with that blessed book too soon, or too well.[1]

This is the goal. Get your son thoroughly acquainted with the Bible. Talk about it as an overflow of your own daily time of learning from the Word. This is foundational. From there, consider a scheduled time of instruction.

I suggest making it your goal to discuss something about every book of the Bible with your sons before they reach school age. That may sound overwhelming, but there is a lot of good material out there that can guide a parent in this kind of endeavor. Being a pastor, I decided to write my own. I called the system I developed *Bible Survey for Kids*. It allowed me to spend a scheduled time with my boys, teaching them the basics of all sixty-six books of the Bible. It involves drawing a simple picture, reviewing the basic characters and truths of each book, and building a timeline chart of Bible history with pictures on three-by-five cards, which are hung on a bulletin board on the wall. Whatever you use, there ought to be a concerted parental effort to teach your sons the basic truths of the Bible. God can use this to build a stable foundation for their forming worldview.

In addition to in-home instruction, I highly recommend a prioritized involvement in a church-based, Bible-centered kids program. There are several; the most popular these days is the nationwide AWANA program, which many churches offer. If this or something equivalent is available in your church, take full advantage of it. The memorization of Scripture that takes place in these kinds of programs will naturally overflow into your home. I know that our whole family ended up memorizing the verses that were assigned to our sons week-by-week. If your church doesn't offer a program like this, what a blessing you would end up being to many families if you prayerfully considered spearheading the launch of AWANA or one of the alternatives in your church.

2. A Praying Home

God will never be a priority in your home if your family is not regularly praying together. Prayer is essential to keeping our minds aware and focused on the presence and supremacy of our Creator. Make sure it is a guarded practice in your personal life and a permeating exercise for your family.

I know it is not hard for us to feel inadequate about our personal prayer time. But because personal prayer is important, allow me a moment or two for us to feel that conviction. Living in the modern world, our default perspective is that we are all "super busy." We may feel busy, and, who knows, we may in fact be very busy, but we have to consider where our time goes and ask ourselves if what we spend our time on is truly more important than the most important things that we so often neglect.

Few things could be more important than prayer. If you are "too busy" to pray, then I think I can say with biblical authority that you are too busy. Something in your schedule needs to be abandoned and be replaced with time in prayer. Jesus was busy—truly busy. He had an important mission and was actively involved in doing all that God called Him to do. He was in demand, and everyone wanted His time.

But Jesus *made time* for prayer. We see Jesus modeling the priority of prayer when "he would withdraw to desolate places and pray" (Luke 5:16), when "rising very early in the morning, while it was still dark, he departed and went out to a desolate place, and there he prayed" (Mark 1:35), and when he "dismissed the crowds" and "went up on the mountain by himself to pray" (Matt. 14:23).

As our personal practice of prayer increases, I trust it will be natural to extend that practice to initiate times of family prayer. God calls us to pray always (Luke 18:1) about everything (Phil. 4:6) and for everyone (1 Tim. 2:1). We have plenty to pray about! So gather your family and pray. Utilize those customary times of prayer (which I hope are still customary for most Christians) like mealtime and bedtime. Even before your son can talk, quiet him down, hold his hands, and talk to God. Before you feed him, before you put him down for a nap, before you lay him down to sleep for the night. Pray. Pray about what is going on in your home, your church, your city, your country, and the world.

We have made it a practice in our family to pray when we hear of a crisis. It might be an email, a text, or a news story. Stop and lead your family in prayer. It might be as you pass an accident scene on the freeway, take a minute in the car to lead your family in prayer. It might even be at the sound of an emergency vehicle's siren, just take a moment and say, "Family, let's pray."

We have also made it a practice in our family to pray when our car is soon to arrive at its destination. When we were almost at the baseball field where my son's Little League practice was about to start, we would take a few minutes to pray for the coach, for the team, for the parents, and of course for our son to be a wise, courageous, and hard-working participant on the team. If we were three or four blocks from church, Mom or I would lead in prayer that my boys would step out of the car and walk into church ready to serve others, look out for others' needs, seek to be a blessing to new people, and learn something transformative and strengthening from God's Word. No matter the destination—on the way to school, the grocery store, a friend's house, the park, or to see the grandparents—let's pray!

3. A Thankful Home

Keeping God the focused priority of our homes is aided by our conscious awareness of God's regular involvement in protecting and providing for our families. It is clear and should be obvious to all Christians that "every good gift and every perfect gift is from above, coming down from the Father of lights" (James 1:17). After all, we understand that God "himself gives to all mankind life and breath and everything" (Acts 17:25), and in Christ "all things hold together" (Col. 1:17). Were it not for God's ongoing involvement in sustaining His creation, we would instantly implode. For "in him we live and move and have our being" (Acts 17:28).

These facts are true for all people. The difference between Christians and non-Christians is that we recognize these facts and give God credit for them. This is why we are a worshiping people. We are the ones who "ascribe to the Lord glory and strength"; we are the families who "ascribe to the Lord the glory due his name" (Ps. 29:1–2). This kind of thanksgiving and praise needs to be a substantial part of our daily expression to God and should punctuate our dialog with our sons. We need to generously model our awareness that if something good has happened, God has been mercifully gracious and is due our thanksgiving. "Thank you God!" may be a simple phrase, but I trust our sons would have to admit they heard it often from the mouths of Mom and Dad, and that it made them increasingly aware of God's involvement in our daily lives.

It has been my routine to not only lead in prayer before we leave the driveway on a trip of any kind, but also upon our return—leading the family in a prayer of thanksgiving when we arrive at that same spot in the driveway. I trust our boys will never forget that mom and dad were thankful for every good and perfect gift, even when our trip may have been peppered with various disappointments or costly mishaps. God is good. He is good all the time to our families, and it is important for our sons to hear us leading prayers of praise and thanksgiving to our gracious Lord.

And speaking of grace, as we lead in prayers of thanksgiving, let's be sure to consistently find our way back to thanking God for the most important provision of all—the forgiveness of our sins through the death, burial, and resurrection of Jesus Christ. This is an important element in providing frequent clarification about the gospel in our homes.

A CLARITY ABOUT THE GOSPEL

As the Bible (and I trust your experience) makes clear, your son will never be able to truthfully say, "I have always been a Christian." Everyone enters the world with a need for regeneration—that new birth and divinely imparted life, which comes when the sin inherent in our humanity, and compounded by our own sinful decisions, is wiped away and we are declared righteous by Christ's finished work.

The previous sentence is a mouthful, and full of deep and profound spiritual truth. It may take several years before your church-attending, verse-reciting son is ready to embrace that truth with a faith-filled and sincerely repentant heart. It is critical that well-meaning Christian parents recognize this.

I know it is out of great love and concern for our sons' spiritual welfare that we are tempted to rush this God-induced work of the Spirit. But we cannot. Any pressure and manipulation will only result in a false sense of assurance. When we push, cajole, or pressure our boys to recite a "sinner's prayer," walk an aisle at church, raise their hand at some evangelistic camp, or sign up to get baptized, we may only be providing them with a reason to turn away from the genuine inner conviction of God's Spirit down the road. Be careful with this.

Of course we want to encourage every step our boys make toward God when they are young. But we also need to understand the kind of "grown-up" life event it is to respond rightly to the gospel. I am not saying that children cannot become truly regenerate Christians—often they do! But often they don't—even if they are raised in God-centered and Bible-saturated homes. To turn from a sinful life of self-direction to a life of submission to the work, will, and word of the Lord Jesus Christ is a huge personal transformation. Yes, it is a work that God sometimes does in the life of a young boy. But for many, these early "moves toward God" stem from immature desires to conform to a parent's expectation, a childish fear of being left out from their parents' eternal home, or a camp speaker's emotional manipulation that would have had him signing up for any number of groups, movements, or organizations.

BECOMING A CHILD OF GOD

To become a child of God not by "the will of man, but of God" (John 1:13) is something that will always involve a few fundamental elements. Encounters with these elements is what we should pray for and seek to continually clarify as our sons grow and mature in their understanding of biblical truth.

1. A Well-Rounded View of God

Don't get me wrong, but in one sense it is unfortunate that the first verse our boys traditionally learn is John 3:16 (i.e., "For God so loved the world that he gave his only Son . . ."). Yes, that is a fantastic and essential summary of God's saving work motivated by His love. But it assumes a lot of foundational truths that many don't learn until much later. In a sense, teaching our boys first about God's love is out of biblical sequence. It's like having someone in high school tell you that "Jennifer loves you!" If I know little or next to nothing about Jennifer, or worse yet, if I imagine Jennifer to be someone she is not, learning that Jennifer loves me will end up being meaningless.

The Bible doesn't begin with God's love; it begins with God's position over us as the sovereign Creator. "In the beginning, God created . . ." (Gen. 1:1). That is where a person's understanding needs to start, and our boys need to learn this right out of the gate. God is the ultimate authority over all things in creation by virtue of His position as our Creator. I often liked to explain this to my boys by reminding them of how they felt about the things they created. They felt a certain sovereignty—an authority or rule—over those things, whether it was a tower they built with Lego blocks or some hard-to-decipher sculpture they made with modeling clay. When they went about displaying (or destroying) it, I would point out to them that they felt a sense of "lordship" over those creations because they made them. From the earliest days, we parents need to underscore God's absolute sovereign authority over the things and people He has made. He is the Potter and we are the clay (Isa. 64:8).

A parent also can make clear that this divine Potter is a perfect, holy, and righteous Potter. Though His very complex pots have rebelled and messed up His creation, He remains holy and righteous. He does no wrong and has a perfect standard for us, which He calls us to keep. The problem, as we all know, is that we don't keep that standard. But the standard is good. As the apostle Paul said, "The law is holy, and the commandment is holy and righteous and good" (Rom. 7:12). From the very beginning, we always want to affirm this with our boys, even when we fall so short of it. The standard remains: "as he who called you is holy, you also be holy in all your conduct" (1 Peter 1:15).

A third foundational truth about the character of God we must consistently impress upon our boys is that our holy God is also a just God. After affirming God's holy standard, Peter adds: "And if you call on him as Father who judges impartially according to each one's deeds, conduct yourselves with fear throughout the time of your exile" (v. 17).

This "old-fashioned" and forgotten virtue of the *fear of God* may be one of the main reasons so many kids grow up in Christian homes devoid of it, and therefore never embrace the grace of the gospel. When we understand the position, perfection, and justice of God, we are truly prepared to understand the gracious and merciful love of God.

This is why a well-rounded view of God cannot be produced on the singular attribute of God's love. Throughout our boys' developmental years, we as parents must train them in understanding that God is the "Boss of us" because He is our Creator. He is a perfect Boss with perfectly righteous rules, He is a just God who punishes sin and rebellion, and thankfully He is also a loving God who has extended grace to contrite sinners and rebels.

2. Conviction of Sin and the Need for Grace

Those facts can be understood as objective truths, but real conversion requires that they are internalized, and that the Holy Spirit produces the conviction that all truly converted sinners have experienced. This may be one of the most difficult realities for modern parents to recognize. Today's moms and dads want to shelter their boys from every negative emotion, and what is more negative than the true feeling of guilt? Yet the apostle Paul is clear:

> For even if I made you grieve with my letter, I do not regret it—though I did regret it, for I see that that letter grieved you, though only for a while. As it is, I rejoice, not because you were grieved, but because you were grieved into repenting. For you felt a godly grief, so that you suffered no loss through us. For godly grief produces a repentance that leads to salvation without regret, whereas worldly grief produces death. (2 Cor. 7:8–10)

Without the tears of truly owning one's sinful rebellion, there is no hope of genuine salvation. As parents we must be much more willing to pray that our boys will get caught in their sins, if not by us or some other human, by God Himself. We must pray that their sense of exposure and guilt they feel before a holy Father will result in indignation about their sin, and will lead them to echo the words of that familiar hymn:

> Amazing grace! how sweet the sound,
> That saved a wretch like me!
> I once was lost, but now am found,
> Was blind, but now I see.
>
> 'Twas grace that taught my heart to fear,
> And grace my fears relieved;
> How precious did that grace appear
> The hour I first believed![2]

3. The Provision of Christ

In Scripture, the gospel presents God as maintaining His justice in dispensing grace toward sinners because of the substitutionary work of Christ. This, our boys should learn early, is the reason we give such central worship and adoration to Jesus Christ. Yes, Jesus is presented to us as fully God, but because He is also fully man, He has selflessly taken the Christian's place before God's just tribunal and incurred the penalty for sin that we deserve. God was willing to treat Jesus, His perfect Son, as though He were the sinners that we are.

As our sons—yours and mine—grow up with a repeated reinforcement of what that transaction provided, we should pray that a day will come when, because of the conviction of God's Spirit over their sin, they cling to the cross by faith—hearing the words "paid in full" on their behalf. When that life-changing conviction comes, we want to be sure they know where to turn in their hearts. We want them to have a well-informed theology that takes them immediately by faith to that place where atonement has been made for their transgressions.

Speak often of the cross, and not always in those familiar poetic phrases that frequently obscure the legal aspects of the transaction. When your son's heart is contrite, he may need more than a lyrical understanding of what happened on that Roman execution rack. His conscience will likely need a more concrete sense of God's justice being perfectly satisfied because someone has suffered the consequences of his rebellion for him. Yes, speak often of the cross, and talk about it in varied and assorted terms throughout your son's childhood.

4. Genuine Repentance

The Bible tells us the repentance that accompanies salvation is much more than being sorry for one's wrongdoing. It is more than being sad about the consequences of one's mistakes. It is more than the embarrassment of being caught in a misdeed. Genuine repentance in both the Old and New Testaments depicts a turning from sin to God (Isa. 55:6–7; Ezek. 18:30–31; Acts 3:19; 26:20). It is an indignation about what sin is (2 Cor. 7:11) and the grief and damage it brings to God. It is a sincere and wholehearted abandonment of continuing in those same things. It is an about-face from a life lived for self to a life that is lived for the One who died for us (2 Cor. 5:15).

Repentance doesn't mean that Christians don't sin anymore (1 John 1:8), but it does mean that the pattern and trajectory of sinful behavior is seriously changed:

> And everyone who thus hopes in him purifies himself as he is pure. Everyone who makes a practice of sinning also practices lawlessness; sin is lawlessness. You know that he appeared in order to take away sins, and in him there is no sin. No one who abides in him keeps on sinning; no one who keeps on sinning

has either seen him or known him. Little children, let no one deceive you. Whoever practices righteousness is righteous, as he is righteous. (1 John 3:3–7)

As someone once said, the repentance that is granted by God's Spirit when we are genuinely converted does not make us sinless, but it does make us sin less. It doesn't mean a truly saved teenager doesn't commit sin, but it does mean he doesn't practice it like his non-Christian counterparts. Recognizing true repentance in a person's spiritual life shouldn't be much harder than recognizing it in his biological life. If someone told you he had "repented" of eating unhealthy foods and was on a new path, no longer eating junk food and fattening desserts, it wouldn't be hard to assess whether his "repentance" was real. Time would tell. His practice would be determinative. If it were only "turning over a new leaf" for a week or two, you'd conclude it wasn't real "repentance." If he, like all frail dieters, had momentary lapses, you'd understand. You'd also see a different kind of "post-repentance" response to that kind of dietary stumbling. There would be a kind of disdain and indignation about his dietary failures, which he never had prior to his "repentance."

So a healthy caution about just any proclamation of your son's spiritual repentance is in order. Not that we don't want to celebrate heartfelt moves toward Christ, but we also don't want to heap on our boys a false assurance about their salvation if their repentance has a human rather than divine origin.

5. Abiding Faith

Like repentance that lasts and has a lasting effect throughout the remainder of your son's life, an accompanying saving faith in Christ is also the kind that endures. Real saving faith is a kind of trust that continues to trust in Christ as the only solution to our sin problem. It is not Christ plus anything else. It is an abiding faith in what God transacted at the cross by having His Son absorb our acts of sin and rebellion; it is the all-sufficient payment and qualifies us to be a part of God's family.

Your son's faith in the saving work of Jesus Christ should transfer

But What About . . .

WALKING AWAY FROM GOD

Although the statistics vary from report to report, it is fair to say that about 80 percent of the "Christians" in America's church youth groups end up walking away from any claim of faith in Christ by the time they hit their twentieth birthday. The Bible says, "We have come to share in Christ, if indeed we hold our original confidence firm to the end" (Heb. 3:14). It doesn't say "we will share in Christ," but "we have come to share in Christ" if we demonstrate an abiding faith in Christ.

Again, the Bible gives plenty of allowance for stumbling saints and times of doubt. But we should note there is a big difference between the stumbling of Peter and the defection of Judas. Both of them proved the reality of their faith (or lack thereof) by how they responded to their episodes of faltering faith. The one God used to advance His cause is in the book of Acts; he got up and was strengthened in his faith after stumbling. The other, the one Jesus called "the son of destruction" (John 17:12), didn't just stumble, but literally "fell headlong" and never got up (Acts 1:18). He proved the absence of saving faith by being the fair-weathered "friend" Jesus so often taught about (Matt. 13:21), and that even the apostle John was able to see through (John 12:4–6).

his trust from anything he can do to make up for his sinful behavior. It is the assurance that Jesus has adequately lived the perfect life in his place and has died a sufficiently painful death for all that his sins deserve. That is a profound kind of faith. It is far more than affirming some facts about God or merely believing the truthfulness of what the Bible teaches. Such abiding faith in Christ can be sustained—even through their college years.

Yet we know many young adults walk away from their faith once they leave home, whether from college experiences or challenges to their faith by acquaintances or coworkers. (See sidebar.) Here is some practical help in this regard. Give your son firsthand experiences and connections with other mature and thoughtful Christians beyond "Mom and Dad"—especially Christian men! Throughout his childhood, open your son's exposure to intelligent, accomplished, and fruitful Christian men. Bring them over for dinner. Take them out to lunch. Allow your son to ask these men questions. Let your son witness rational and thought-provoking discussions between you and these men. Your son will undoubtedly benefit from interacting with strong examples of Christian faithfulness.

Every Christian parent of a son wants that boy to come to a place of genuine repentance and faith. Keep praying for him, teaching him the Scriptures, discussing your Christian worldview, modeling the truth, and clarifying the gospel. Both my wife and I prayed persistently that our boys would come to saving faith in Christ. And by God's grace, both of our boys have professed a genuine relationship with Jesus Christ and are currently showing what appears to be evidence of genuine repentance and an abiding faith. We praise God for this, and I pray that you will be able to say the same of your boys.

Here are a few points of spiritual common sense to apply the principles and concerns just mentioned.

Never Make Light of Sin

In our culture it is easy to laugh at the things that put Christ on a cross. Do your best to make it taboo in your home. This will affect the movies you allow to be watched in your home. It will be tested by what makes you laugh. Your boys are watching. Be ruthless about keeping in view the terrible price of human sin and rebellion, and work to never make light of sin.

This will also impact the way you respond to transgressions in your own home. Do your best never to say, "It's okay" or "No problem" when there is a confession of some wrongdoing against another family member. Model the reality that sin is never "okay" and is always a problem. Biblical forgiveness doesn't overlook that; instead it finds a way to grant forgiveness. Teach your kids by example to say, "I forgive you" when there is someone who says, "I am sorry."

A home that truly fears God, in the appropriate and biblical sense, will always be sensitive to sin. Members of that home won't make heroes out of reprobates, and won't celebrate things that grieve God. See sin for what it is, and teach your boys to do the same.

Make Church Participation a Top Priority

Make sure your sons are actively involved in the church. Do this without hypocrisy. Be sure you are faithfully and actively involved as well. The church is the spiritual community God has ordained to nurture your family's spiritual life. Pick the best one within reasonable driving distance and get plugged in. Be done with the excuses and realize that your boy's experience at church is formative in his understanding of Christianity at large.

If you are half-hearted about your church, hit-and-miss in your attendance, or are loyal to a substandard church that is not really preaching God's Word or challenging you or your family in their spiritual growth, make the hard decisions and get the members of your family where they need to be. These kinds of decisions may be painful at first, but over time you will look back and wonder why you waited so long to make the move.

Model the Priority of Church When You Travel

One of the most overlooked blunders we parents can make is what we do on Sunday mornings when our families are on vacation. When your boy sees you bail on church services, because you are not home and it is not your church, is it really any wonder that he learns to bail on church when he moves out of the house and is no longer in his home church?

Get yourself and your family to church when you are out of town. I know it is tempting to use all the current technology to peek in on your home church service when you are in some distant city, but you are teaching your boys something by that simple compromise. Show them that you are motivated to look up that city's best Bible-teaching church, and that you are eager to jump in the rental car and join in the worship of Christ with your brothers and sisters of another town. I find that we always leave these spiritual vacation adventures glad we made the investment, sometimes with great ideas about how to improve our home church, and sometimes just thankful for our home church. Most importantly, I have taught my boys something by my example: no matter where God might move me, His church will be my priority.

Require Spiritual Disciplines as Long as You're Paying the Bills

I frequently get questions from parents about their spiritually disinterested son. "Should I force him to read his Bible?" "Should we make him go to church?" "He doesn't really want to go to that church camp; should we require him to be a part of it?" Yes, yes, yes! That's the short response. My medium retort is: "What do you do when your son says he doesn't want to do his math assignment?" "What is your response when he doesn't want to go to school?" "How do you handle it when he says he doesn't want to go and take his exams?"

"Well," you might say, "I don't want him to hate the Bible or church the way he is learning to hate math or math class." But math is important, so you keep on him. You make him because what he is begrudging to learn is important for him. Right? When my boys were little, before they had a chance to hit me with, "I don't want to go" but were hesitating, I'd say, "Boys, there are things we do in this family: everyone showers, brushes their teeth, puts on deodorant, reads the Bible, goes to church, and serves in church. As long as you live here, that's what you'll do!"

That may sound old school, but so be it. If you are paying the bills you have the right to make the rules about what the occupants of your house will do when it comes to the Bible and church. Put your boys in a place where they will encounter the truth—even if they are unsaved and unwilling. As you would if your children rebelled against some other important value in your home, firmly and lovingly require it for their own good.

Get Your Kids Reading Good Christian Books

From the earliest days we have read good Christian books to our boys. As they got older we required them to read important Christian books. Of course, the Bible is the unrivaled and most important Book that our family is expected to read. Before our boys could talk, we read to them. We'd read to them a variety of good children's Bibles, and then supplemented that with an assortment of age-appropriate books on Christian themes and Christian biographies.

Even into their high school years, our breakfast table was the time and place my wife would read another chapter of a good Christian book, which was chosen according to the comprehension level of our youngest. The commentary and discussion that followed would often be over the head of our youngest, but the breadth of exposure to Christian doctrine and Christian missionaries proved to be time well spent. While they plowed through their breakfast each morning, my wife would chip away at another good title. What a great way to double-up! Much better than wasting time with the TV or reading the back of a cereal box. Get them reading the good stuff by reading to them.

It is my prayer that by doing this, along with a composite of the other strategically planned spiritual investments we have walked through, you will find that you have trained up your boy in the way that he should go, and by God's grace "even when he is old he will not depart from it" (Prov. 22:6)!

A HOME THAT BUILDS GODLY MEN

The tallest skyscraper in San Francisco is going up as I write this chapter. This new addition to the South Market District, Salesforce Tower, promises to exceed 1,000 feet, easily surpassing the iconic Transamerica Pyramid, which is "only" 853 feet.

Last year the construction crews attempted to ensure that this new record-setting tower would be around for many years in this earthquake-prone part of our country. To do so they spent eighteen hours on a cloudy Sunday afternoon pouring what seemed to be an endless quantity of concrete into a huge crater on the Mission Street construction site. When it was all done, it was reported that this foundation consisted of an unprecedented forty-nine million pounds of concrete poured into a five-million-pound steel lattice of rebar.

All this to remind us that a foundation is important, especially in a turbulent world. Your son needs a stable launching pad—which comes through a strong and sturdy home life. That sentence can make a parent say, "Ugh!" if he or she is tuned in to the many imperfections present in every human household. The goal of this chapter is not to discourage you with some impossible standard, but to motivate you to do what you can to shore up your son's home experiences so that his overall childhood experience will motivate him to become a productive, influential man for Christ.

THE PRIMACY OF YOUR MARRIAGE

The first human relationship to be created was between a husband and a wife. God did not create the parent-child relationship and then add a spouse to round out the household relationships. The marriage relationship was designed to be primary. As we have already noted, the marriage relationship was also designed to last a lifetime, in contrast to the parenting relationship, which was to endure until the child went off to be joined to a spouse in marriage. The marriage was also to be primary in importance. The language in Genesis 2:24, along with the rest of what the Bible teaches on marriage, makes clear that the "holding fast" to one's spouse is a kind of connection that is to be valued as the supreme earthly relationship in the family. The relational bond God designed for marriage then, we could say, was first in time, first in duration, and first in priority.

That says a lot about the way a home ought to look and operate. The function of the members of a household ought to seek to clearly demonstrate the primacy of the marriage relationship. Just putting it in those terms can serve as a wake-up call for many Christian homes. Even though I introduced this chapter with the observation that our sons do best when they are sent out into this world from a strong home, and therefore from a home with a strong marriage, we need to make sure we don't see the focus on our marriages as a means to an end. Yes, it is true that the future path for our "men in the making" is being set for them by what they observe in the relationship between Mom and Dad, but let us for a few minutes just consider the importance of marriage for God's sake, not our boys' sake.

Reconsider the Solemnity of Marriage

God certainly did not have to create marriage as we know it, but He did. The Lord obviously decided that this sacred, intimate, lifetime bond between a husband and wife would be a demonstration of the type of relationship that would bring Him glory and reflect His character. He wanted it, as both the Old and New Testaments explicitly tell us, to be a billboard displaying the way God loves and enters into covenant relationship with His people. The frequently recited parallel between Christ and the church, and husbands and wives, should not be seen simply as a biblical way to teach Christians how to have better marriages, but as Paul writes, "This mystery is profound, and I am saying that it refers to Christ and the church" (Eph. 5:32). In other words, marriage itself exists primarily because God chose to reflect the profundity of how He relates to the church—His chosen, elect people.

If that doesn't elevate your respect and esteem for what your marriage is, I don't know what would. If you are married, you are in a relationship that needs to be admired and valued, not because it is perfect or filled with good feelings every day, but because it is the unique and hallowed covenant connection between human beings. With that said, it is no wonder it is under such tremendous attack in our modern era. Here is a divinely designed institution crafted to display something of God's love for His redeemed people, having endured for millennia throughout human history, yet in our day finds Satan boldly seeking to change its rules and sully its reputation.

Speak Highly of Marriage to Your Boys

One way to show respect for marriage is to be done with all those jokes about our boys not dating until they are thirty. This is particularly in vogue for Christian parents of girls. In the last few months I can recall at least four godly Christian couples talking about their daughters, and jokingly referring to shooting any boys that might be romantically interested in their girls. It is sure to get a laugh, but consider the cost. The anti-dating, anti-marriage rhetoric that is built into so much of the Christian culture's thinking (much of which stems from the parents' defeatist projection of their sordid dating failures on their kids) certainly contributes to our church kids reflecting the sad anti-marriage statistics of the rest of the world.

Not only is our culture giving up on marriage in droves, but those who still choose to engage in this sacred covenant relationship are putting it off way past what is verifiably healthy for their future children (more on that and the whole topic of dating and marriage in chapter 8). Marriage is entered into later in life now than it has ever been before, and the age for getting married the first time is fast approaching thirty. Tragic how the fulfillment of the wish for our boy to put off marriage quickly turns to desperate prayers for our grown offspring to find a wife and start a family. Yikes!

In contrast, let us speak highly of marriage to our boys from the outset. Talk positively to your son about his future marriage. Talk about the great blessing it is to be married. Take your cues from God's inspired parenting proverbs and echo these sentiments often:

He who finds a wife finds a good thing and obtains favor from the LORD. (Prov. 18:22)

An excellent wife is the crown of her husband. (Prov. 12:4a)

House and wealth are inherited from fathers, but a prudent wife is from the LORD. (Prov. 19:14)

In those times when you find yourself thanking God for your spouse, purposefully share your thanksgiving with your son. When you are blessed by something your spouse has done, be intentional about declaring your joy to your boy. Not only does that put on display the best of this sacred relationship, but it also provides a tremendous sense of security in your son's life.

Remind Your Boys Your Spouse Comes First

As counterintuitive as it may seem, make sure your boys know that your spouse is your first priority. This doesn't seem like a good idea if you wanted to affirm and encourage someone were it any other

But What About . . .

LACK OF RESPECT FOR MARRIAGE

At some point your sons may wonder if marriage is worth it, or even if you care about your spouse (their mom or dad). Here's why. In 1960, 84 percent of working-class Americans were married. Today you can invert those numbers—only 48 percent of working-class Americans are married.[1] The number of children born to unwed mothers has gone from 4 percent in 1940 to 40 percent today[2]—despite the advent of several birth control methods. Not to mention that our culture no longer considers divorce the serious breach of a solemn vow as it once did.

Marriage is under attack, but you and your spouse can launch a counterattack before your children and others as well. Speak well of marriage whenever possible, and live as though it is the sacred and prioritized relationship God intended it to be. Speak highly of your spouse—and your love for her (or him) before your children. Be done with the "ball and chain" jokes before coworkers and neighbors, and rid your conversation of any demeaning lines about your spouse that can always get a laugh.

Most importantly, hold marriage in the highest regard, praying daily not only for the strength and health of your own marriage, but also for the marriages of your friends, the marriages at your church, and for your boys' future marriages.

relationship, but in your parenting relationship it is exactly what your boy needs to hear. If you want to provide the kind of security and reassurance that every child inherently needs, then it is time to see the wisdom of telling him emphatically that he is *not* your number one priority.

This is modern parenting heresy, I know. But oh well, it is the truth—or at least it should be. Because God designed marriage to be first in time, first in duration, and first in priority, when your son is in a household that adheres to God's design, he will flourish! Your boy is strengthened and prepared for his future when you demonstrate not only with your words, but also by your daily decisions, that your covenant partner is the primary earthly commitment in your life.

When this is flip-flopped, or affirmed only in our words and not with our lives, we will create the bane of the modern family—namely, the child-centered home. Entitled, self-indulgent, bratty, self-absorbed sons are cultivated in a home where they are convinced they are the number one priority. We can witness the effects of this in every nook and cranny of our society. Walk into a supermarket, a hotel lobby, a shopping mall, or sadly, many church lobbies and you will witness kids who rule, and big people who seem to be tagging along for the ride. All these children are missing is a golden crown affixed to their brow. They are the unrivaled sovereigns of their domestic domain and they know it.

This is the sinful and perverse reality for far too many homes, and for many who claim Christ and say the Bible is their guide. But you can search the pages of Scripture and never find anything that remotely supports the kingly role many little boys assume in today's families. Godly Christian homes are described as dignified and well managed, with children who are faithful and submissive to their parents, not ruling the roost as though they are the center of their domestic universe (1 Tim. 3:4; Titus 1:6). Of course the training of our children to achieve this domestic equilibrium will involve a good dose of loving yet firm correction, which we will get into in the next chapter.

Invest in Your Marriage

A marriage that becomes the bedrock of your son's enriching childhood will certainly require a regular investment of your time and resources. One of the staples of a husband and wife investing in the marriage is the simple and consistent practice of a date night. I can't point to a chapter and verse in the Bible that mandates it, but it is hard to imagine that a marriage in our busy world can be a prioritized and valued relationship if there are not regular times on the calendar set aside and guarded for one's spouse.

Your relationship with your spouse was likely initiated and cultivated by putting dates on the calendar and keeping them. Your relationship will be maintained and enhanced by continuing the same practice. I know, I know, you live with your spouse and you see him or her every day. I met my future wife when I was in high school. We had classes together. I saw her every day. I'm sure that classmates is all we would have ever been, were it not for making dates and investing in each other. Yes, you see your spouse every day, but to cultivate and deepen your relationship with your marriage partner you must get those dates on the calendar and keep them.

As parents of a young boy, this can be a challenge. But you need to be up for the challenge and make it happen. We briefly touched on babysitters in the first chapter. I can say that date night is one of the most important weekly reasons to share the care and oversight of your son with a grandparent, friend, or trusted babysitter. Even when they cry as you are on your way out the door, power through the separation anxiety in your own heart, and say, "Goodnight, I'm off to date your mom!" I can remember my tearful sons pulling the "you're-killing-us-here" attitude when it was time for me to leave on my weekly date night. I would often get down on one knee, pull their little faces toward mine and say, "I'm going out tonight to date your mom, and I expect that when you are a daddy you will take your wife out on a date every week no matter how much my grandkids tell you not to!" It was my way to try to humorously impress upon their little minds the primacy of marriage—both mine, and one day theirs.

Of course there is a lot more that could be said about your investment in your marriage. If you are clueless as to how this can be done, pick up a good book on Christian marriage, or simply be bold enough to sincerely ask your spouse, "What can I do to make you a greater priority in my life?" And when you get the answers, be sure to put those things into practice in a way that reverberates throughout your home. Make sure your boy can truly sense that you are committed to loving, serving, and prioritizing your covenant marriage partner.

THE MODELING OF MARITAL ROLES

It is likely that your son will be called to be a husband, and will need to reflect the God-given role that his dad is now working to fulfill before his eyes every day. Dads, this puts the pressure on you to make sure you are providing him a good and godly example of what Christian leadership in the home is supposed to look like in the modern world in which we live. Moms, you too should feel some appropriate pressure in this arrangement. Your son will learn a lot about how a good and godly wife functions in a marriage, and how she interacts with her husband. You, moms, will set a standard of what a Christian wife should be. Your son will draw on what he learns from you to choose his own wife.

Biblical Headship

If this heading is an offensive combination of words in your mind, I am not sure I can help you a whole lot in this brief section. I would certainly encourage you to research and seek to understand the perfect arrangement of complementary roles that God has devised and commissioned for every marriage relationship.[3] But assuming you are appreciative of God's perfectly logical and impeccably wise reminder that any two-headed creature is monstrous, then you must recognize that Dad needs to model the loving and sacrificial leadership role that every family needs.

Dad needs to lead. He needs to plan. He needs to assume an ultimate responsibility for the welfare of his home. Far too many "Christian" homes have passive males at the helm, who are leaders in name only. Of course, I am not calling for dictatorial decision-making; I am simply observing that far too many dads show a great deal of care, creativity, and passion in their leadership at work, but as soon as they step through the doorway of their house, they plop down and act like big kids. In the absence of male leadership in the home, Mom will by necessity pick up the mantle, which unfortunately undermines and frustrates a hundred lesser aspects of a functioning marriage and home. When Dad abdicates his leadership role, the entire family will suffer. And perhaps worst of all, the pattern of passive husbands and checked-out dads will likely repeat itself in the next generation, as your son learns how a "Christian" home is apparently supposed to operate.

Dad, I encourage you to take the responsibility and to feel the obligation of leading your family into the future. Get your arms around the finances and start to save for the eventualities that lie ahead. Strategize about how to best meet the needs of each family member. Think about next summer, next Christmas, next year. What needs to be repaired, shored up, strengthened, or replaced? Discover the long-term needs for each family member, make a plan, and get to work making their lives better. Don't be autocratic, harsh, or totalitarian. You can still be decisive, strategic, and forward thinking. Model for your son that a Christlike leader leads with an insightful heart and, even at great personal cost to himself, looks out for the good of those he leads. This is true biblical headship.

Biblical Submission

Just as husbands may shake at the H word featured in the past few paragraphs, wives may cringe at the S word. I know submission is out of fashion and is disdained as archaic, but let's all grow up and recognize that all the condescending rhetoric against God's design for wives is nothing more than another attempt by our lying enemy to steal from us the ideal of a fulfilling married life.

This is married life as it is intended to be. Now I confess I married a very strong and intelligent woman. Carlynn is an effective leader, a powerful conference speaker, and a tough-minded biblical counselor. But if you get a chance to talk to her, ask her if biblical submission to your husband is a blessing or a curse. There is no doubt she will praise God for the depths of His wisdom and knowledge (see Rom. 11:33). She also will tell you—as could a million other strong and intelligent wives throughout church history—that there is no better arrangement, and no more advantageous an arrangement, than for a woman to lovingly submit to the leadership of her husband.

You may, as many do at this point, object that this arrangement works only when the husband is a good and godly leader. Granted, that does make things less frightening. But as many Christian wives can attest (Carlynn included), even when one's husband is less than wise, learning to navigate the bumps and turns with your husband, while still fulfilling your God-given role as a submissive wife, is a far better thing than ditching God's plan for the world's plan.

Wives, model for your sons how a loving and supportive wife behaves. Seek your husband's leadership and counsel. Cheer on his leadership and openly express your trust in his love, care, and provision for your family. Fight the temptation to be a worried and anxious wife. Cultivate your ultimate trust in God's sovereign oversight of your life and family. Consistently pray, privately and publicly, for your husband. Compliment him freely. Let your boy regularly hear you praise your husband for the good he does for your family. Let your respect and admiration for the man you married be a familiar memory your son takes into his adult life. Not only is this good and right, but it may also make a world of difference in who ends up becoming your daughter-in-law.

AFFIRMING YOUR SON'S MASCULINITY

Run the clock forward several years in your mind and picture your son as the strong husband and capable father you pray he will become. That kind of confident, masculine strength needs to be fostered now, little by little, month by month, and year by year. Cheer on every meaningful step of courageous and sacrificial leadership. Your boy may be a boy now, but you are raising him to be a man, so any move in the direction of bold, resilient, thoughtful leadership and influence should be celebrated.

Our world won't help you with this one. Men and almost every expression of their masculine leadership are mocked in sitcom scripts and TV commercials. Unless it is the primal, vicious, gratuitously violent shoot-'em-up movies, strong men are out, and weak, passive men are in. Even how educators treat our boys is decidedly against their masculinity and expressions of strength.[4] So be reminded that if your husband is not praised by you for showing initiative, strength, and courage, he probably never will be. Affirm your husband before your son.

Clearly I am not saying every boy needs to be a football star. Expressions of biblical masculinity are not narrowly defined as the actions of a middle linebacker. Your boy may never wear a jersey or hit people for sport—that is not the point! Cultivating the future men of the next generation will include all types of personalities and temperaments. But all men in God's economy are called to be brave, strategic, and resolute. Our young men dishonor Christ's plan for their lives when they grow up content to be passive wimps, who have been given no equipment or encouragement as men to "fight the good fight of faith" (1 Tim. 6:12), or to stand up in their generation enabled to "share in suffering as a good soldier of Christ Jesus" (2 Tim. 2:3).

WHEN THE HOME IS BROKEN

Up to this point I have addressed the issues concerning your boy's domestic launching pad as though it is intact. If so, praise the Lord! Pray that it will stay that way. But if, like so many homes these days, yours has been fractured by divorce, and the application of these principles seems a greater challenge because of shared custody and visitation schedules, remarriage, and perhaps blended families, then read on.

The bottom line is this: do what you can. When it comes to putting these things into practice, do what is possible. If you are parenting without a male role model in the home, then you'll have to enlist the help and influence of a godly male Sunday school teacher or youth group leader, a Little League coach, grandfather, or uncle. You may feel like you are raising your boy with one hand tied behind your back. That may be an apt analogy for the reality of what you are up against, but pray and work to become proficient and as skilled as possible with that admitted disadvantage.

Throughout the process, be sure to avoid two critical and common mistakes. First, put away your anger. It is easy to brood and stew that your domestic life is far more challenging than that of the family across the street. It may be, but your anger doesn't help (James 1:20). Let the anger go and get to work on the situation you find yourself in. See the source of this kind of anger as stemming from your transgression of the Tenth Commandment. You have been called to never covet (Ex. 20:17). Stop agonizing about the advantages you don't have, and purpose to pursue the will of God in your present situation. You can't change the past, but God has promised to walk with you into the future. That leads me to the second common mistake.

Don't lose heart. Perhaps you read that last paragraph with a clear conscience. You're not mad, but instead you're glum. Realize that doesn't help either. Worse than unhelpful, this attitude will keep you from optimistically pursuing God's best for your son. When God tells us Christians, "I will never leave you nor forsake you" the next line reminds us of the attitude that should accompany such people: "So . . . we can confidently say, 'The Lord is my helper; I will not fear; what can man do to me?'" (Heb. 13:5–6). If this is true (and of course it is), then we need confidence while parenting in a broken home, not despair, despondency, or discouragement.

Remember you are not totally alone; your Partner in this man-raising endeavor is God Himself! Be biblically optimistic about what God can do in the underdog situations. Let us confess with the apostle Paul: "But he said to me, 'My grace is sufficient for you, for my power is made perfect in weakness.' Therefore I will boast all the more gladly of my weaknesses, so that the power of Christ may rest upon me" (2 Cor. 12:9).

BUILDING FUTURE MEN IN DAILY LIFE

Let's conclude with a few ways we can help our boys move toward maturity as confident leaders. Perhaps some of these approaches can spark your own creative thinking as parents to nurture growth to biblical manhood.

The Outdoors

Without trying to turn this into a guide for creating macho men, let me suggest that there are some great lessons to be learned by getting your boys outside, conquering fears, and learning to exercise dominion in an outdoor context. I'll confess that I don't like camping. I want my nights on a vacation to include an elevator and an ice machine. With that said, I did my childhood share of tent sleeping and backpacking, and I did value the confidence that was bred in learning to survive in the "elements."

Surely this will be read by some who are in a much different setting than mine, prompting some to take their young boys out for an adventurous wild boar hunt. Okay, fine. But even if you are a city slicker like me, you might consider the old-fashioned Friday overnight camping in the backyard. I remember doing this with my boys in my tiny Orange County tract home yard, and I can say it certainly brings a rustic experience to your sons' lives that sleeping in their bunk beds never would. There are also a variety of scouting, camping, or outdoor adventure groups available for your son, if not as a regular participant, at least as a periodic experience.

Exploring the neighborhood park, the bike trails, or traveling to a national park are all great experiences for your young man as he learns to conquer his childhood fears and becomes increasingly competent in new and uncharted environments.

The Sports Fields

As I alluded to earlier, not every child is a gifted athlete. In my family, my brother was the sports star; I gravitated to music and art. Yet I am very thankful that due to my brother's influence and my parents' provision, I was allowed to join a few sports teams, and had the childhood experience of going to practices, gearing up for game day, competing, winning, and losing. These were good experiences— character-building experiences. I wasn't great at any of the sports, but even riding the bench on my seventh grade basketball team taught me something that I have benefited from as a man.

I am reminded of the biography of a great British sports star, the talented Cambridge cricketer C. T. Studd, who came to Christ over a hundred years ago and then went on to change the world of Christian missions. His biographer wrote:

> C. T. never regretted that he played cricket, although he regretted that he had allowed it to become an idol. By applying himself to the game, he learned lessons of courage, self-denial and endurance, which, after his life had been fully consecrated to Christ, were used in His service. The man who went to be

an expert cricket player later went all out to glorify his Savior and extend His kingdom.[5]

As a parent who was never a sports star, I still required my boys to join a sports team. I didn't really care which of the major sports they played, I just wanted them to have the beneficial experiences that come from playing. I was more than happy to have them drop out after a season or two, knowing that the rigors of practice, the expectation of the coaches, and the pressure of game day would wear on them; but I also knew those demands also would play a role in the formation of who they would become as men. As it happens, they both excelled in several sports, and ended up reminding me of the kids who kept me riding the bench through much of my childhood.

The Stage

I add the stage to the important places our boys learn some of the skills of becoming men, not because it was my preference as a young musician, but because I have found that standing up in a recital or at a performance of some kind is also an experience that teaches courage, determination, and resolve.

Learning an instrument as a child is an obvious way to lead your boy into this experience. As with sports I realize that there is a gifting and talent that some children just don't have when it comes to music, but I required it of my sons anyway. They didn't have to become musicians, but I did want them to learn to read music, experience the tedium of practicing an instrument, and have the personal involvement in sitting on a platform and performing before an audience. I was more than happy for my boys to drop out of their junior orchestra or band after their first or second year, but both enjoyed the experience, gravitated to other instruments, and are now proficient enough to competently sit in to assist in leading worship at church when needed.

The stage can also be a place for acting and speaking. Many

churches provided the opportunity for our boys to get up on stage during a Christmas pageant or Easter play. This was another mandatory exercise for my boys. Even if they had no chops to sing solos (which they didn't), I wanted them to try out for the speaking roles, learn their lines, and participate in the production. While neither of my boys went too far with this, I do believe that reciting lines on a stage with a microphone buoyed their confidence, which now pays off as both of my boys have become proficient young teachers of God's Word, mostly unfazed when standing before hundreds of teenagers to preach the Bible.

QUELL THE REBELLION OF HIS SINFUL HEART

An hour of observation in the church nursery or any local daycare center should dispel any illusion that children are born with a bent to do what is right and an aversion to do what is evil.

On the contrary, as the Bible affirms, we should be quick to attest to the truth that kids are natural-born sinners. It is easy to nod at that fact as long as it's someone else's bratty kid, but as parents we find it much more difficult to give our hearty agreement when it comes to our own children.

NATURAL-BORN SINNERS

We can never become truly loving parents until we work to eliminate this built-in blind spot: our boys, just like us, are sinners. Our God is so concerned about holiness and so offended by sin that even when it concerns His own redeemed and adopted children, their sinful thoughts, words, and actions cause Him pain and grief (Eph. 4:30–31) and raise His parental concern. How ungodly it would be for us to allow the affection for our sons to blind us to their rebellion. How unlike our Father we would be, were we to ignore their sin and pretend it is not a serious problem.

I say we cannot truly love our children without this sensitivity, primarily because sin has consequences in daily living and in how God is impacted. Think for a moment how much better it would be for our boys were they to be trained to say *no* to sin and *yes* to what is good. This was the Lord's benevolent concern for His children, when He observed their good response to His instructions in Moses's day: "Oh that they had such a heart as this always, to fear me and to keep all my commandments, that it might go well with them and with their descendants forever!" (Deut. 5:29).

One reason we should be sure to notice and be internally grieved by our sons' sin is because it "reap[s] corruption" in their lives and in the lives of others (Gal. 6:8). Some with a high view of the gospel of grace may object at this point. Isn't this attempt to train our boys to keep God's rules legalism, moralism, or some other Christ-dishonoring "ism"?

PRE-CONVERSION RULE KEEPING

As noted in chapter 2, our boys do not enter this world saved, forgiven, and indwelt by God's Spirit. They must each individually, at some point in their development, come under a true conviction of the Holy Spirit, experience genuine repentance and sincere faith, and cast themselves on the gracious redemption provided for them in the substitutionary death of Jesus Christ. This is all of grace, provided completely by the merciful drawing, forgiving, converting, and adoptive work of God.

If we were to address people on the topic of doing good as it relates to obtaining salvation, we would say to non-Christians that their "righteous deeds are like a polluted garment" before a holy God (Isa. 64:6). No matter how good they may feel they are in comparison to other sinful people, their best efforts "fall short of the glory of God" (Rom. 3:23), and that they become justified before God only "by faith apart from works of the law" (v. 28). If, however, we were talking to redeemed Christians about doing good, we would remind them that though they cannot earn God's gracious acceptance, that His grace is always motivating us and "training us to renounce ungodliness and worldly passions, and to live self-controlled, upright, and godly lives in the present age" (Titus 2:11–12), and that when we Christians engage in what is "good and right and true" it is "pleasing to the Lord" (Eph. 5:8–10).

This is a very important distinction: good behavior as a means to gaining or keeping a relationship with God is *offensive* to God, but good behavior done to please God by those who are in relationship with Him is *prized* by God.

When you think about the institution of the family, your role as a parent, and the pre-conversion state of your young son, don't confuse a discussion about justification and salvation with your role as a parent in promoting good behavior in his life and disciplining his bad behavior. This is your role. That should be your expectation. There is no need to fear that you will create a little legalist by establishing and upholding the expectation that your child must obey you, his parents. When you make and enforce righteous rules you are fulfilling your duty as a parent in the divinely established institution of the family. This is the appropriate concern of God for all children in any household (Prov. 20:11).

RETHINKING ALL THE RULES

As with all authority, there comes responsibility. Every authority is ultimately answerable to God, and the Lord would always have us exercise our authority with great care.

Yes, you get to make the rules for your boy's day-to-day life.

75

Because the Bible clearly says, "Children, obey your parents in every-thing, for this pleases the Lord" (Col. 3:20), how he responds to your rules has an effect on how God feels about your family. When your boy disobeys your rules, he is displeasing God, but as the lawmaker, you don't want to displease the Lord in the rules you make. The Bible also says, "Fathers, do not provoke your children to anger" (Eph. 6:4). That is easy to do when your authority is wielded in a frustrating and exasperating way.

What I am about to say can be easily misunderstood and even dismissed as unbelievable by those who know me and my wife, but it is really the way we have approached our role as the ones who make the rules in our home. We are firm believers in making as few rules as possible! I know this may be hard to believe by those who know us because we are typically viewed as law-and-order disciplinarians. I suppose we are, but it is precisely because we want the rules in our home to be kept that we are careful not to overload our children with too many of them. Instead, we have found it helpful to legislate a few big rules and then work to be consistent about enforcing them.

For instance, we want our sons to know that it is nonnegotiable and that they are required to respect their parents, be kind to others, demonstrate self-control, not complain, and respond promptly to our call. I know that these kinds of "big rules" leave us open to the negotia-tion that is sure to follow when we believe one of them has been vio-lated. But I think that this post-infraction discussion has been good to help our boys think through the kinds of behavior that are acceptable and the kinds that are not.

The bottom line is go easy on the legislation. Don't load your boys up with a ton of little rules about every situation they might possibly find themselves in throughout the week. Remember that everything you establish as a house rule, God takes seriously and will expect your boys to take seriously too. Leave room in your legislative leadership for the kind of latitude that you may find builds a thoughtful skill in their developing conscience, to truly consider what is profitable and detrimental, good and bad, better and best.

CORRECTION AND DIRECTION

Legislating is one thing, but it is the enforcement of the rules that is most demanding and unpleasant for us as parents. But enforce we must. It is our God-ordained role as a mom or dad. After warning us about not provoking our sons to anger, Ephesians 6:4 tells us to "bring them up in the discipline and instruction of the Lord." These are two very important words: *discipline* and *instruction*. The word *discipline* in the original language of the New Testament refers to an unpleasant response by a parent when a child does wrong, in hopes of steering him away from his disobedience. I like to call this simply, *correction*. The word "instruction," on the other hand, is the word used in the New Testament to depict the exhortation or coaching of a parent to show a child the right way to go, often on the heels of their wrong behavior. I call this *direction*. Correction and direction are two sides of our enforcement of the rules. Before I get into how these can be effectively practiced by Christian parents, let me remind you of the urgency the Bible gives us for faithfully engaging in the hard work of correction and direction.

The Perpetual Motivation

A permissive parent needs only to consider the long-term effects of a child who rarely receives correction and direction to change his or her lenient ways. The Bible has that long-term perspective in view when we are reminded that "a child left to himself brings shame to his mother" (Prov. 29:15). It may not be today or tomorrow, but eventually your heart will break over a son who has not learned to restrain his sinful desires. When God tells us that the "wages of sin is death" (Rom. 6:23), it ought to send a chill down any parent's spine and instill in us a sense of urgency and responsibility. God even charges us as being complicit in the corrupting consequences that befall our sons when we fail to restrain them. Consider the implication of this proverb: "Discipline your son, for there is hope; do not set your heart on putting him to death" (Prov. 19:18). Who sets their heart on putting their son to death? The answer: a shortsighted parent who fails to diligently provide correction and direction to their boy.

As I said, all of this spells love. We enforce consequences and provide coaching in right behavior to our sons because we care about them, just as God cares for us. The Bible draws the parallel for us and reveals God's motive when He disciplines us.

> And have you forgotten the exhortation that addresses you as sons? "My son, do not regard lightly the discipline of the Lord, nor be weary when reproved by him. For the Lord disciplines the one he loves, and chastises every son whom he receives." It is for discipline that you have to endure. God is treating you as sons. For what son is there whom his father does not discipline? If you are left without discipline, in which all have participated, then you are illegitimate children and not sons. Besides this, we have had earthly fathers who disciplined us and we respected them. . . . They disciplined us for a short time as it seemed best to them, but he disciplines us for our good, that we may share his holiness. For the moment all discipline seems painful rather than pleasant, but later it yields the peaceful fruit of righteousness to those who have been trained by it. (Heb. 12:5–11)

That is a long passage. If it is familiar to you, you probably skimmed it. If so, you ought to go back and read it again slowly and thoughtfully with your boy's face in your mind's eye. God loves us and won't look the other way when we rebel against His rules and instructions. If we love our boys, as this passage assumes we do, we wouldn't consider doing any less. Applying unpleasant consequences for wrongdoing is non-optional. To *not* firmly and resolutely correct and direct our boy is sin.

Consider the parenting failure of the Old Testament priest, Eli. His tragic story is often concealed in our memories by the surrounding Sunday school lessons about the young Samuel. Every Sunday school graduate remembers the story of the boy Samuel, who kept hearing a voice in the night calling to him. Thinking it was Eli, he continued to run in and ask what Eli wanted, until Eli finally grew wise to the possibility that the young Samuel was going to fulfill the role of a prophet, and told him to say, "Speak, LORD, for your servant hears" (1 Sam. 3:9). Then, of course, the Lord revealed His truth to Samuel. Millions of churchgoers remember that, but relatively few can remember what the Lord actually said to Samuel:

> Then the LORD said to Samuel, "Behold, I am about to do a thing in Israel at which the two ears of everyone who hears it will tingle. On that day I will fulfill against Eli all that I have spoken concerning his house, from beginning to end. And I declare to him that I am about to punish his house forever, for the iniquity that he knew, because his sons were blaspheming God, and he did not restrain them. (1 Sam. 3:11–13)

The message: Eli was a bad father. His boys were sinful, and he did not restrain them. The chilling thing about that charge against Eli was that he had certainly *confronted* his boys about their rebellion (1 Sam. 2:22–25), but apparently that was all he did. He didn't *restrain* them. How many times have we all seen parents acknowledge the bad behavior of their kids, maybe wag their finger and tell them, "That's not good, Johnny" or "Bad boy" or "No, no!" but that's it. The 1 Samuel passage doesn't tell us what more Eli should have done, but the rest of the Bible clearly does, even before we get through the pages of 2 Samuel.

Proper Correction

When God refers to picking up the parental role in the life of King David's son, Solomon, He speaks of the kind of correction that the rest of the Bible reiterates. Unfortunately, the way the words are translated into English from the original Old Testament Hebrew leaves most modern readers wide-eyed and appalled. But here it goes: "I will be to him a father, and he shall be to me a son. When he commits iniquity, I will discipline him with the rod of men, with the stripes of the sons of men, but my steadfast love will not depart from him, as I took it from Saul, whom I put away from before you" (2 Sam. 7:14–15).

If there is a passage that sounds like child abuse, there it is. But before you picture for the word "rod" a bar of steel rebar from a construction site and for the word "stripes" the sort of lacerations on Jesus' back when He was being beaten by the Roman soldiers, you had better get the biblical definitions and the context in view.

The application of unpleasant consequences for a child's disobedience in this passage, and every other instructive biblical passage to parents, is a disciplinary act applied in "steadfast love" and not anger or retribution. The stripes are admittedly a vivid depiction of the act of swatting, but not a beating, or even a reference to leaving marks on one's body. The "rod" referred to here is the Hebrew word, *shebet*, used throughout the Old Testament to depict a small stick. The ancient shepherd is described as carrying a "rod and staff." The staff is the long stick that is often as tall as the shepherd and traditionally represented with a crooked or hooked end on it. By contrast the rod is a small stick tucked into the belt of the shepherd, which can be used as a tool to count the sheep, a poker to prod an unresponsive lamb, a disciplinary device to rap a wayward sheep on the nose, or even as a defensive weapon to protect the flock from predators.

In Isaiah 28:27 the word "rod," from the Hebrew word *shebet*, describes a tool in an ancient kitchen used to crush cumin seeds in the preparation of a meal. This might rightly bring to mind something on the order of a wooden spoon, like those found in a jar on the kitchen counter. That is a long way from the iron bar or "rod" of rebar that might have immediately come to mind. With this appropriate definition and the context of a loving parent applying unpleasant consequences for a son's misdeeds, we can now read how the Scripture speaks to parents.

The Bible says, "Do not withhold discipline from a child; if you strike him with a rod, he will not die" (Prov. 23:13). In other words, your application of a painful consequence for your boy's rebellious act will curtail his rebellion and save him—spare him, redirect him—from the "death" that would inevitably come from unbridled and increasing sin. The next verse drives the point home: if you strike him with the rod, you will save his soul from Sheol (v. 14). *Sheol* is the word used to describe the abode of the dead, the grave, and the end of life. Of course, it is not just physical death that is in view. The point made when the Bible says, "the wages of sin is death," certainly includes a variety of negative consequences that come from sinful acts.

What this might look like will vary depending on the situation and the age of our boy in a minute, as we will see. For now, let us recognize that our parental job of providing unpleasant consequences for bad behavior is a loving action that moves beyond words to real-life penalties. These diligently imposed consequences have the effect of restraining our boys from the terrible things that would surely and eventually come into their lives, were they to continue down their sinful path without being corrected.

Direction

Bringing up our sons in the "instruction of the Lord" or being "directed" in a righteous path as I have called it, is a kind of coaching and forthright counsel that shows our boys a better way than sin. If correction is seen as the unpleasant work of imposing negative consequences for sin, direction can surely be seen as the much more positive, affirming, and enjoyable work of instilling what is right. But you can be sure that it is still work. Actually it takes so much work that far too many seemingly tired and busy Christian parents neglect it. But we really can't afford to. It is impossible to adequately deal with the rebellion of a young sinful heart by correction alone.

I realize that only the regenerating work of the Holy Spirit can rewire and internally transform the human heart. But much like the Golden Retriever that is successfully taught not to jump up on your guests but to sit quietly while you serve steaks to your friends, your son can be successfully trained to practice the "upright" conduct that we learned God expects of children (Prov. 20:11). Your faithful instruction and active direction can aid your boy in living out a kind of childhood that the Lord reasonably expects of young men.

At the heart of providing the "instruction of the Lord" is making sure that the Word of God is a constant diet in your son's life, as we discussed in chapter 2. Be sure that he is thoroughly acquainted with the truth of God's Word as early and often as possible. In the section on the Bible-saturated home, I talked about Bible surveys, personal Bible reading, good Christian books, and church programs that can augment your son's biblical input. But understand that truly directing our sons in the instruction of the Lord will require more than an intake of biblical data; it will necessitate biblical discipleship. In other words, the knowledge of truth, while essential, isn't enough! Truth always demands a response, and we must help our boys to know how to put the truth into action. This is where the book of Proverbs, again, provides us with excellent insight about the training of lives, not just the filling of heads.

Consider how the Proverbs of Scripture are in many cases the application of how a young man ought to put the principles of God's truth into action. It will say far more than simply: "Don't be sexually promiscuous!" These instructions from a parent to a son (5:1; 6:20; 7:1) guide him to think practically about the pitfalls and vulnerability of being naïve about sexual sin (7:6–9), the hazards of girls who flatter

(5:3; 7:5), the peril of those who lack modesty (7:10), how a young man's honor is at stake (5:9), and how his reputation will ultimately be sullied (6:33).

This is just one example based on a single biblical topic that shows how parents are to thoughtfully coach their sons to walk the path of righteousness. This example obviously involves a topic for maturing sons, but even if the coaching is for our very young sons and their inclination to throw tantrums, know that true biblical discipleship and effective training in upright conduct must always be practical and include wise direction and specific suggestions for avoiding temptation, and learning to prioritize what God values.

Before you think that you have to be a Bible scholar or trained in counseling methods to effectively raise your son in the instruction of the Lord, let me encourage you that any ordinary Christian has what it takes to make this happen. As the apostle Paul said about the Roman Christians (a church he had never personally visited), "I myself am satisfied about you, my brothers, that you yourselves are full of goodness, filled with all knowledge and able to instruct one another" (Rom. 15:14). They were not perfect, as the correctives throughout the letter make clear, but because they were growing Christians who were bearing fruit (which I trust is true of you), he was confident that they were apt to instruct their peers. Certainly I can say the same for the Christians reading this book, who are seeking to instruct and direct their sons.

We, as modern Christian parents, have the advantage of the complete inspired library of God's revelation in our language. In addition, we can go online today to access or acquire digital Bible study reference tools that organize the themes and topics of the Bible by subject. There are also many Bible software tools and print resources, which can assist us in locating what God has to say in Scripture on just about any general theme our young men might have to deal with. Add to that the years of experience we have to draw from regarding how we have implemented God's truth, and we should be able to assist our sons in the practical steps they ought to take to fight their way through the challenges of being a young man in the twenty-first century.

If and when you are stumped, gather with other Christian parents at your church to glean from them the ways they have sought to train their sons in the instruction of the Lord concerning the issues you are facing in your parenting. Consult your pastor or other church leaders to accumulate wisdom on the topic you are wrestling with. And of course, read on to discover in this and other sound Christian books how Christian leaders have trained their children.

THE DISCIPLINE SESSION

When our sons fail to follow the instruction of the Lord and rebel against our parental direction, it is time to correct. At that point we will have to move from simply accepting the responsibility to correct, to actually doing something that will provide real correction. Effective correction will differ depending on the age of our sons, as well as the kind of rebellion that has taken place. But we should recognize "all discipline" becomes effective in redirecting lives away from sin when it is "painful rather than pleasant" (Heb. 12:11). That unpleasant experience imposed by loving parents is to be tied to the sinful behavior that would otherwise prove to be costly and destructive.

Avoiding Pain (The Baby Years)

Think of the way God builds this principle into the physical world. Even prenatally your son's body is wired to send unpleasant and in some cases extremely painful sensations to his brain when he does something that, if continued or repeated, would be destructive or damaging. If your son were to poke his thumb in his eye or clamp his jaw down on his tongue, his brain would send a painful sensation that is translated as: "Don't do that!" This kind of association of pain with actions that are harmful is a pattern that will be employed in a million situations throughout his baby years (under age two), just by living in the physical world. This association will train him not to repeat actions that, though at the time he doesn't realize it, are in fact detrimental to his well-being.

Your infant son has always been a fast learner when it comes to this cause-and-effect experience. Unpleasant sensations ensure that education. Even the so-called "strong-willed child" learns quickly that poking himself in the eye hurts badly and that he had better become self-controlled and skilled at avoiding that action. He couldn't explain it even if he could talk, but he learns well enough the truth that thumbs and eyeballs don't mix. He then proceeds to live with the advantage of not doing something that will damage and perhaps destroy God's intention for his eyesight.

Now think about that cozy moment you might be sharing with your infant son on the sofa, when he suddenly reaches out and sticks his finger in *your* eye. What ought to happen in that moment? Is he too young to learn not to do that? Well, it didn't take him long to learn to keep his fingers out of his own eyes. Or what happens when he clamps his strong, little, pre-dental gums down on some part of your body? Remember that he has already learned that clamping down hard on a part of his own body is to be avoided, because it comes with painful consequences.

These are just two of the hundreds of situations at the early onset of your boy's life, when you have to manufacture an unpleasant experience in his life. I realize this is not a moral transgression, but it is a physical "transgression," which, if continued, will cause physical damage. In these situations there must be for him what is already familiar to him—an association between painful sensations and actions to be avoided. Depending on the disposition and sensitivity of your infant boy, the manufactured experience may vary. A very sensitive son may only need the unpleasantness of a disapproving look and a strongly worded "No!" to successfully get the idea that Dad's eyeballs are off limits. (I, by the way, didn't have any sons like that, though I've heard they do exist. At the very least, in situations like that, my two sons needed the added unpleasant impulse of a firmly gripped arm or a tightly held finger for a brief moment or two.)

With the consistent application of these unpleasant experiences, we quickly discovered we could eliminate our baby boys' grabbing (of our faces), biting (of their mom), and scratching (of their dad)—almost as quickly as they had learned not to inflict pain upon themselves. This cause-and-effect learning experience is easily transferred from a child's physical exploration of the world around him to his willful defiance that can crop up much sooner than parents-to-be might imagine.

Spanking

I can remember the "changing table wars" that took place with both of our sons. One was a little stronger willed and noncompliant than his brother, but they both tested Mom and Dad with this early on. Both sons quickly came to recognize that a little cooperative time on their changing table would result in a more comfortable life for the whole family. But apparently they believed that changing their dirty diapers was supposed to happen on their schedule and not ours. Well, that is not how parental oversight is designed to work. When it was time to change, it was time to change. Our expectation was obedience and compliance as we attended to something that was certainly for their own good. It was not time for rolling over, or twisting and arching their backs.

When a firm grip on their hand and a stern "No!" wouldn't make the impression required, we employed our kitchen *shebet*, a small wooden spoon kept in a jar on top of their dresser. A small and quick application of the *shebet* to their outer thigh in association with a clear "No" and "Lay still," immediately widened their eyes and success-fully made the point. Over a few days, as that point was consistently impressed upon our young sons, their only twisting and squirming was

But What About . . .

IS SPANKING CHILD ABUSE?

When properly applied, spanking is an expression of love for your child. The action should always be motivated by love, and it is *never* to be done in anger. I understand that some of the defiant actions of our sons may instantaneously raise our blood pressure and stir our anger. When they do, we have to take a few minutes to get our pulse rate down and our attitude in check. In the rare situations when the literal *shebet* [small rod or stick] is employed, it must be done by a mature parent who has his or her emotions under control.

Our avant-garde culture may categorize any kind of spanking under the heading of "abuse," but the loving yet unpleasant application of the *shebet* is anything but abusive. All discipline is unpleasant. But "abuse" has to do with a misuse of something that is excessive and creates a bad effect. The Bible is clear: failing to enforce unpleasant consequences on our errant children is the ultimate excess of indulgence and causes the worst of all effects.

Some argue spanking teaches kids to be violent, and certain websites cite published reports to prove that. But that is not the case! The "spanking" the critics so often write about is not the "spanking" that the citizens of heaven are talking about, which is derived from biblical instruction, a correcting done with love and care. Even secular observers are beginning to see that so much of what has been reported on in opposition to "spanking" has overlooked the loving and measured *shebet* sessions many of us employ. In the past decade several studies and reports defend the practice of spanking.[1]

the playful wrestling on the couch with Mom and Dad. The association of something sufficiently unpleasant with their decision to disobey successfully corrected the behavior, and there was never a need for those nylon restraint straps I have seen attached to modern changing pads.

That description of a typical battle of the wills between a parent and young son on a changing table, and how we solved it, may be immediately repugnant and even shocking to some modern readers. "That sounds like the angry, abusive, violence-producing, antiquated practice called spanking," some might say. Well, it may fit the dictionary definition for what has been known as "spanking," but that's about the only word in the sentence that can be properly employed for what I am talking about. If today's lexicon defines spanking as angry, abusive, and violence-producing, then I can assure you that what I am referring to couldn't be further from that reality. The motive and attitude count. Done correctly, *spanking is an act of love*. Really!

Whenever I teach on this topic, particularly in the progressive state of California, I have people approach me and say, "You are advocating for something that is illegal!" Again, so many have listened to the alarmist noise of our culture, but actually have no clue of what they talking about. Even here in crazy California the "spanking" that I am referring to is legal. Section 300(a) of our state's Welfare and Institutions Code clarifies that though, of course, it is illegal to "cause serious physical harm" to our children, "'serious physical harm' does not include reasonable and age-appropriate spanking to the buttocks where there is no evidence of serious physical injury."[2]

I was once counseling a couple in my office on this topic, when the mother challenged me on the legality of applying the *shebet* in appropriate matters of parental discipline. I was frustrated and making little progress on convincing her. Ready to give up and move on, I thought I would try one last tactic. I picked up my office phone and dialed the number for the local police station that I had in my top drawer. I reached a police officer, who was apparently working the front desk of our city's police station. I had no idea who he was or how he might respond. I asked if I could put him on the speaker phone and ask him a simple question. He said, "Sure." I proceeded to identify myself as a local pastor sitting with a couple from my church, and said, "Is it illegal to spank our children?" Hoping he'd lend some convincing support to my counsel, he surprised me with his enthusiasm. "Oh, please would you?" he said. "Would you please spank your children? I am so tired of having to deal with the grown-ups in our town who never had loving parents who were serious about correcting their boys' behavior by applying the paddle to their rear ends!" Point made—at least to them. They may still think he was a plant and it was all a set up. But it wasn't. Just a random call to a cop who knew from experience that "folly is bound up in the heart of a child, but the [*shebet*] of discipline drives it far from him" (Prov. 22:15).

Practical Creativity in Quelling Rebellion

Literally applying the *shebet* to the posterior end of our boys is effective for only a season when our sons are young. By the time our boys are five or six years old, the unpleasant consequences usually need to become more and more creative. I learned this in practice when I started giving my boys an option. Our strong-willed boys had long since transitioned to *shebet* sessions from Dad instead of Mom. (That became necessary as they started to express very little trepidation when Mom sought to employ the wooden spoon.) I had them graduate to a little wooden paddle, which I had them watch me craft in the garage for just that purpose. It had proved effective for many a *shebet* session. But once I said, "Okay, son, you've disobeyed your mom and now that I am home you need to have the *shebet*. But I will give you the option. I can give you the four swats Mom has said you earned, *or* I will take away your dessert tonight and you will have to go to bed a half-hour early." Once he consistently started choosing the *shebet* swats, they stopped being an option. I realized that for him it was significantly more unpleasant to incur the sacrifice of his ice cream cone and his playtime that night after the bath, than to experience the admittedly firm *shebet* swats from dad. Knowing that the unpleasant association needed to make the strongest impression, a variety of creative consequences kept the birch *shebet* gathering dust on the top shelf of the closet.

Be creative. You know your boy. You know what will make the point clear that his rebellion or defiance is not worth it. Realize that the older he gets, having his posterior sting (even if it really stings), will become less of an unpleasant consequence than having to clean the garage for an hour and a half, or not being allowed to watch tonight's baseball game, or being prevented from an anticipated Friday night gathering. Be *reasonable* and *proportional* based on the infraction, but realize that the unpleasant consequence has to make its impression.

If your boys are young and the *shebet* is still the effective means of correction for a serious act of defiance, then be sure you explain the reason for the unpleasant consequence. Make certain they understand the cause and effect of why this is happening. And most importantly, be sure to reaffirm your love for them when the session is over. Tell them you love them and that is why you want them to learn to avoid sinful and rebellious actions. Remind them that God's *shebet* is bigger than yours, and that you want them to avoid the serious "sowing and reaping" that exists in the grown up world.

Remind them as well, that you know what it is like to sin and reap the painful consequences. Tell them that ultimately our sin and its consequences remind us of the gospel and the great thanksgiving Christians have that the eternal consequences of sin, which are far worse than any earthly consequences, were absorbed by Christ. And that your continual prayer for them is that one day they will come to the place of sensing their need for the forgiveness that comes when we acknowledge all of our sins before God, sincerely turn from them, and trust in Christ's willingness to be punished for them in our place.

Even if you think they are too young to grasp those truths, there is no better time to get our boys familiar with the components of the gospel than when they are grappling with their own sinful choices and considering the damage those choices have caused.

MAKE HIM SWEAT EVERY DAY

You may not think you are familiar with the Estonian carry in the *eukonkanto* races, but I'll bet you've seen videos of this bizarre competition. Every year or so the news will present us with pictures of this unique race, which apparently originated in Finland. *Eukonkanto* means "wife carrying" in Finnish.

Yes, eukonkanto is the "sport" of wife carrying, and it has gained in popularity in America after beginning in Finland and being promoted in Estonia. Competitors will sling their wives over their shoulders, most of them with the wife inverted and draped over the husband's back (known as the "Estonian carry"), as the men run a course like frantic madmen down dirt roads, over hay bales, through water pits, and over log barriers. Eventually the winning couple crosses a finish line to claim the prize of the wife's weight in beer. Wacky!

The last time I saw a news clip of this zany steeplechase, I couldn't help but think of many modern parents who do their best to restrict and restrain the natural frenetic hustle and bustle of their little boys. You might hear that those accused of fearful, restrictive over-parenting are sometimes called helicopter parents, due to the effect of all that hovering, but they might better be described as eukonkanto parents.

I'm pretty sure I won't coin a new descriptive phrase, but I do hope the mental image of a mom or a dad trying to continually hold back the energetic running and jumping of their little boy will provide us with a worthy picture of our actions.

Of course, there are times our boys need to sit still and be quiet. They certainly need to learn appropriate self-discipline, and be taught how to exercise reasonable self-control to get through a variety of situations when it is disruptive and inappropriate to be a loud, squirmy, sweaty little ball of exuberance. But I would have to agree with those who have chronicled our society's bias toward standards that favor the general temperament of little girls over little boys.[1] The behavior standards, daily schedules, and general expectations of most educational institutions—and sadly of most churches and Christian families—are rarely suited for the naturally squirmy, fidgety, and rambunctious disposition of male children.[2]

HE IS A BOY

In God's perfect wisdom His creation has been purposefully filled with the reflection of the complementary features that exist within the persons of the Godhead. The Lord decided that there should be throughout His creation a variety of examples of the equal worth and value that exists within the persons of the Trinity, yet with clear and notable distinctions between persons. These distinctions are to be celebrated and joyfully embraced. Just as the Son and Holy Spirit exist as coequal persons possessing all the glory of the Godhead, yet there are complementary distinctions in how they function and the roles they fill.

The most beautiful reflection of this equal-yet-distinct principle has been given to us in the creation of male and female. While Christians should always be quick to insist on the coequal value and incalculable worth of every human life, they should also be enthusiastic to affirm and celebrate the dissimilarities in the way God has crafted men and women. Humanity's two corresponding genders matter very much to God. The intrinsic contrast between these two genders is something that brings glory to God.

Putting human personhood in those terms should make obvious the logic of why homosexuality is consistently presented in the Bible as a distortion of God's created order. But more than that, this divinely purposed distinction helps us understand why any attempts to ignore or blur these gender differences are also prohibited by God. Consider the ancient command that men should not wear women's clothing and women should not wear men's clothing (Deut. 22:5). This is far more than a prohibition against a sexually motivated transvestism, or cross-dressing. It should remind us of the command to the early church to maintain the culturally distinct clothing of the first century that distinguished men from women in the worship service (1 Cor. 11:2–13). There was nothing about sexual impulses in view in those instructions. The Bible is simply reiterating the importance of gender distinctions that bring glory to God among His people. And while the secular culture in Corinth at the time was casting off any concern about gender distinctions, God called His church to maintain them.

Christians often quote the line, "What God has joined together, let not man separate" (Matt. 19:6). Those words of Christ refer to the divorce of a man and wife that God has joined in the sacred bond of marriage. But consider the principle in reverse. It could also be said of many things: "What God has set as distinct, let not man confuse." As Jesus said at the top of the discussion in Matthew 19, "he who created them from the beginning made them male and female" (v. 4). Male and female distinctions are not to be disregarded. The multitude of associated masculine-feminine distinctions are to be embraced, applauded, celebrated, and maintained.

The celebration of our boys being boys should begin day one. Our confused and rebellious society will tell us that "this line" is cultural heresy, but we don't answer to the pundits of our world. We answer to our Creator, who has established and ordained these God-glorifying differences. Let us be glad our boys are distinctly male. Sure there are plenty of understandable differences to be found among young men. We may have an experience like Rebekah in Genesis 25, who had Esau, described as a "skillful hunter, a man of the field," and then gave birth to Jacob, who was said to be a "quiet man, dwelling in tents" (v. 27). But for all of Jacob's quiet nature, his masculinity was never to be confused with the femininity of his wife Rachel or his daughter Dinah.

No, your boy might not be the high school quarterback. He might not even have the athletic prowess to try out for the team. But men are designed by God to develop that uniquely masculine gallantry that might find its expression in the Saturday morning chess match or on a stage leading his math team to a district championship. That masculine ambition to lead, fight, protect, and explore has been fueled by the unique levels of testosterone which God has washed his cells in before he was born. You need to rejoice in that maleness, make room for its expression, and be ready for all the implications that come with it.

BRUISED OR BUBBLE-WRAPPED?

We have reached an almost comical point of seeing this generation's ultra-concerned parents employ every imaginable means to protect, shield, and shelter their children from any conceivable harm. It has become so ridiculous that in a single day, I stumbled upon a satire website claiming to sell plastic bubbles to protect our kids with pods "available in a variety of sizes, with prices ranging from $499 (young toddler) to $799 (college age)."[3] I then moved on to read a liberal secular blog with an article entitled: "Stop Bubble-Wrapping Your Kids! How Overprotection Leads to Psychological Damage."[4] And then I read from a book in my own library authored by a highly respected evangelical conservative with a chapter title: "Are We Raising a Nation of Wimps? A Coddled Generation Cannot Cope."[5]

It is hard to imagine any subject on which the satirists, the liberal psychologists, and the conservative theologians could all agree. But in effect they do. Yet I look around in the real world and most people completely ignore their unambiguous call to stop being such overprotective parents. In everyday life it seems that most parents operate with the ultimate priority that any risk of bumps, bruises, stitches, or skinned knees will not be tolerated. As so many other writers have pointed out, the effects of shielding our children from physical pain, emotional disappointment, or unpleasant experiences are reaping an overwhelming load of unintended consequences. It is time to accept a measure of those physical dangers, which are inherent in raising a rollicking, adventurous, active little boy.

Prepare yourself. There will be trips to the ER. You will raise a boy who enters adulthood with a few scars from his childhood stitches. He will probably have memories of friends signing his cast after he broke a bone as a kid. Your only option to eliminate these likely possibilities is to become that overprotective, over-parenting, ultra-restrictive, domineering person who will exasperate your son. You will end up suppressing an important developmental process of trial-and-error, cause-and-effect, risk-and-reward that your boy needs if he is to become a mature and productive man.

MOM SAID "NO" / DAD SAID "OKAY"

In most homes during the early years of raising your boys, the "Mom-said-no / Dad-said-okay" clash is bound to happen at least once a week. It happens most often when the issue on the table carries some inherent risk of physical harm. "Can I have a skateboard?" "Can I try out for the team?" "Can I play on the trampoline at Brian's house?" Expect this marital dilemma. And remember that part of the reason God designed parenting to be a partnership, was to include a masculine risk-taking man and a feminine nurturing woman, because there is need for both as you raise your kids. The problem in our culture, which has produced the massive increase in pampered, wimpy, bubble-wrapped kids, comes down to how these clashes are resolved.

In most cases, a dispute about whether Johnny will or will not be allowed to do this or that, is determined by Mom's veto. If Mom senses it is dangerous, Mom wins, not 60 percent of the time, but in my observation over 90 percent of the time. If Mom can't get comfortable about the danger involved, then, even if Dad thinks the risk is reasonable, his vote is overturned. Dad soon thinks, *Well, I guess Johnny could get hurt, and if I were to press my opinion and he does get hurt, I'll feel terribly guilty.*

Allow me to appeal to you Moms for a moment. You should not win in every one of these disagreements. To become the man that God intends him to be, decisions will necessarily have to be made that you didn't feel completely sold on. God has designed for your husband to provide an influential voice of leadership in the decisions you make about what you let your son do.

I am not saying that everything Dad is comfortable with should be agreed upon in every case. You and he may start just with the goal to split the difference. Consider making it your goal to purpose to say "yes," even when you are uncomfortable, at least as many times as you know your husband has agreed, "Ok, we will not let him do it" (knowing his thoughts typically are *I think it would have been fine*).

Oh, and if and when your son does get hurt in that thing you forced yourself to allow and you want to scream, "We never should have let him do that!"—don't! Most of these bumps, bruises, and even stitches and casts are used to shape your son's character. I am not advocating you raise a careless daredevil. I'm all for reasonable precautions. I am all for a helmet when he rides the skateboard. I want reflectors on his bike. I expect him to wear shin guards when he plays soccer. But I don't want your boy's budding masculinity to be stunted because he has been quarantined in a plastic bubble.

HE'S NOT GOING PRO (I'M PRETTY SURE)

I am clearly advocating for allowing and even encouraging your boy to engage in activities that will involve some risk of physical injury. One arena of childhood where that danger undoubtedly lurks is organized competitive sports. Participating on sport teams is a legitimate, even important, experience that can reap many benefits in the maturation of your son's character. With that said, please remember he's not going pro! I can be pretty sure of that. Both of my boys played Little League baseball in a fairly competitive part of Southern California. Both were good players on their respective teams. One made the all-star team for the district. Neither played in high school. If they had been good enough and dedicated enough to play in high school, the NCAA reports their odds of playing in Division 1 college baseball is 7.1 percent,[6] and earning a single paycheck from a Major League Baseball organization is one half of one percent.[7] Those, by the way, are the best odds. Football, basketball, and soccer odds are even worse.

These stats are given not to discourage you or your boy from doing his best in childhood organized sports, but simply to put his participation in perspective. The rigors of practice, workouts, and being pushed by coaches can be an ideal way for your son to expend much of that pent-up, testosterone-fueled boyhood energy in a constructive way. The winning experience can provide instructive opportunities to learn to win with grace and humility. Striking out, stumbling in competition, and losing games can be the settings in which your boy learns to control his emotions, restrain his words, and learn from his mistakes. But to see this as an on-ramp to a college sports scholarship and later a pro career is a big mistake.

With all of sports' benefits, your boy's participation on a sports team is secondary when compared to his supremely valuable participation in the body of Christ or the spiritual disciplines of Bible reading and prayer. If you doubt that, go back and reread chapter 2. Or better yet, reread these two key Bible passages for a fuller perspective:

Train yourself for godliness; for while bodily training is of some value, godliness is of value in every way, as it holds promise for the present life and also for the life to come. (1 Tim. 4:7b–8)

Every athlete exercises self-control in all things. They do it to receive a perishable wreath, but we an imperishable. (1 Cor. 9:25)

And when your family is missing church for another travel-ball tournament, or you're deciding to have your son skip the church's kids summer camp for his sport's team training camp, or you're declining an invitation for his participation on a missions trip or a youth leadership team because your sights are set on his Division 1 college scholarship, remember how we started our thinking when we discussed his spiritual trajectory: "For what does it profit a man to gain the whole world and forfeit his soul? For what can a man give in return for his soul?" (Mark 8:36–37).

Sadly, many parents have sacrificed the spiritual welfare of the souls of their kids at the altar of athletics. Don't place sports above their spiritual needs. It is not worth it—even if they earn a free ride to college, or break all the odds and make it into the limelight of career athletics. Having personally known a handful of successful professional Christian athletes, they would all tell you that exchanging the spiritual development of your son for chasing after what they acquired in their sporting careers is never worth it.

Organized sports? Sure. Making sports an obsession and a consuming priority? Never!

YOUR BALL OF ENERGY

Our boys are born to move. They are full of energy. They are loud. They get dirty. They don't like sitting still. They'd rather grunt than talk. They'd rather wrestle with you than hug you. They are frenzied and frenetic. Their attention darts here then there like a pinball machine. Many—no most—would be labeled hyperactive. There are times this energy needs to be corralled, but wise parents will be careful to employ their spiritual common sense to give appropriate outlets for the way God designed their boys. Here are a few of my suggestions.

Make Him Sweat

Make him sweat every day. Literally. My wife and I made it our goal to try and see those little beads of sweat on the foreheads of our boys. If it was six o'clock and we hadn't yet seen that familiar mix of dirt and sweat running down the temples of their little boy faces, we'd take them outside to run around, throw the football, climb a tree, or whatever it took for them to experience that tuckered-out feeling we discovered every boy needs. Everything went better in our home—at dinner, at homework time, at bedtime, at just about every other time—when our boys played outside long enough that day to work up a sweat.

When they were toddlers, it seemed my wife was making up games, tasks, and all kinds of creative challenges to get them to physically expend the pent-up energy that God had implanted in their little bodies. In our electronic age, when most parents are quick to turn on a movie to occupy their boys or hand them a screen to engage their minds, we must work all the harder to purpose each day to get our boys outside to a park, a playground, or a jungle gym. We have to plan to get their bodies moving more often and for longer periods of time.

Feed Him Right

What your boy eats every day makes a difference in how he functions, how he feels, and even how he thinks. Like anything else, this concern can be taken too far. I have witnessed some parents become obsessive fanatics in their attempt to enforce good eating habits in their children. That kind of extremism can cause an unnecessary exasperation in your boy's life. But good eating habits taken too far is certainly not the norm, not even in my corner of health-conscious Southern California. Most families do not eat well. The Centers for Disease Control reports that our kids are twice as likely to be obese than we were as children, and adolescent obesity has quadrupled in the past thirty years.[8]

These facts are true not only because our kids are more sedentary (which we must change!), but also because we are feeding them poorly. We don't restrict their food choices the way most of our parents restricted ours, and our decisions as to what to feed them are too often dictated by their childish preferences, and not by our authority and wisdom as parents. Our poor dietary choices often become another encumbrance to our boys' natural energy and exuberance. They need good fuel for all of that God-given energy. We don't want to contribute to a sluggish, lethargic, and frustrating childhood, because we could never say no to their immature appetites, and we never enforced a pattern of learning to eat nutritious foods.

Teach Him Restaurant Manners

Speaking of food, let's think for a minute about the restaurant experience with your boy. You don't want to be "that family" with the screaming kid who runs around the tables making everyone's dining experience a bad one. You don't want to, and as a Christian you shouldn't. "As you wish that others would do to you, do so to them," Jesus said (Luke 6:31). As cute of a cut-up as you might fancy your boy to be, I can assure you he is not as entertaining to most of the customers in the restaurant. So help with proper restaurant manners by being prepared. You never wanted a bratty boy interrupting your dinner before you had kids, and now you need to be a considerate parent by making sure you can channel your young boy's kinetic energies in the restaurant.

My wife and I never went to a sit-down dining establishment when our boys were little, without bringing along our "restaurant-only case of toys." While all the grunting, yelling, and running around had to be postponed for the run to the car in the parking lot, our box of gadgets, crafts, and die-cast airplanes were faithfully supplied to give a modified outlet for those times our boys needed to be occupied. And if the dinners went long (as they often did in my line of work), one of us would excuse ourself with our boys for a quick run around the building or a fast climb of the tree in the corner of the lot.

Allow for Daily Loud Times

Our rambunctious boys were loud. We wanted to make sure they had some time during the day to be as loud as they were inclined to be. All of this was to give an outlet that would be regular and expected so that they could learn in alternate times to sit quietly through a worship service, a restaurant, or when we were entertaining guests in the living room.

It wasn't uncommon to have older adults comment on how well-mannered, quiet, and respectful our boys were in their presence. I would laugh on the inside, and if my boys were in earshot of the compliment, I would smile and wink at them with a look on my face that read, "They have no idea!" Of course they weren't quiet. It might have been just a half-hour ago that the music in our house was cranked up and our boys were yelling or drumming or singing as we got the house ready for our guests. Our boys learned the restraint of being quiet when it was called for, because they knew their loud times were expected, frequent, and encouraged.

Tantrums

When we think of loud outbursts and young male aggression, tantrums come to mind. These angry, uncontrolled outbursts of frustration are every parent's nightmare. They often happen at the worst times and in the most embarrassing places. Even when they take place at home, they are a test of our own patience and self-control. With boys these tantrums can be so wild and chaotic they can become outright scary. As parents our job is to calm the situation, not to escalate it. In certain settings we need to move our boy out of the room and to a private place for him to get a hold of himself and settle down. In every case we need to stay calm and keep our composure so that we can be agents to restore his composure.

The middle of the tantrum is not the time to debate, negotiate, or hand out disciplinary consequences. There may need to be some discipline later for the angry outburst, but when his frustration erupts the only agenda item is to help him restore his self-control. Some settings require that you immediately hold him and hug him, others that you isolate him and allow him to regain his composure alone on his bed, still others that you rub his back and calmly exhort him to get it together. When it is over, it is time to help him understand his own anger in an age-appropriate way. Often it will involve the enforcement of some discipline for the words or actions that his anger has caused. But all of that should wait until after the wave of aggression has past.

My point in bringing up the dreadful tantrums now is to remind us that often we contribute to these outbursts, sometimes by failing to provide enough outlets for pent-up energies, at other times because of our poor scheduling of sleep, and sometimes because of our failure to provide the right kinds of nutritious foods at the right times. After all, even you, with an adult dose of self-control, are a tantrum candidate when something irks you after being holed up in your office all day, with terrible sleep the night before, and a gut full of junk food.

6

INSTILL A MANLY WORK ETHIC

Imagine your boy playing on the high school football team. Now imagine the coach during the week: he only talks to the players about the relief of getting a break during halftime, the fun of doing postgame interviews for the school newspaper, the good times to be had on the bus rides to away games, and how to make the most of Friday morning pep rallies.

That coach certainly wouldn't be the coach of a winning team. And it's likely he wouldn't keep his job for a whole season.

Football coaches need to prepare their players to play football. That's what the athletes have signed up to do. That's why a team has been assembled. Sure, there may need to be some instructions from time to time about all the ancillary events and activities that go along with being a football player, but the main thing the coach is called to do is to prepare the boys to be skilled, disciplined, and hardworking players on the football field.

As parents, you and I are coaches. We are called by God to prepare our boys for life. Our boys have been crafted by God to bring Him glory by exercising dominion over a segment of God's creation. They will fill a role in this world as workers, spending more than half of their waking hours giving themselves to specific tasks, which not only earn them a paycheck but also bring honor to Christ. Read the following words with your son in mind, knowing that one day he will be employed like the rest of the adult world, expending his time and energy in a specific vocation:

> Whatever you do, work heartily, as for the Lord and not for men, knowing that from the Lord you will receive the inheritance as your reward. You are serving the Lord Christ. (Col. 3:23–24)

Imagine your boy, employed to serve the Lord Christ as an accountant, an architect, a pharmacist, a pastor, a computer systems analyst, a construction worker, an insurance agent, a physical therapist, a web developer, an orthodontist, a missionary, a mechanical engineer, a paramedic, a loan officer, a real estate agent, a graphic designer, a schoolteacher, an electrician, or a financial planner. Imagine him at his position day-after-day, engaged in the work that God has called him to do.

Now consider yourself as his coach years before he assumes his position. It is time to assume the thoughtful responsibility of getting him ready to serve our great King at his future job.

THE BLESSING OF WORK

"Work is work," my dad once told me when I begged him to allow me to apply for my first official job. "It won't be easy," he warned, knowing that the thought of earning a paycheck was alluring to a young tween. My dad was right, though I hardly needed his speech that day, having learned from earlier experiences that doing "jobs" around the house and in the yard was always more arduous than I had initially imagined.

The Bible explains that all of the pain and toil associated with productive work is a part of the specific penalty on sinful humanity. "Cursed is the ground because of you," God told our first parents. "In pain you shall eat of it all the days of your life" and "by the sweat of your face you shall eat bread" (Gen. 3:17, 19). It is precisely because of this unpleasant experience that people commonly view work as a curse. But this is not how we ought to view it, nor is this the impression we dare give our boys.

The pain associated with work stems from God's curse, not the work itself. The dominion exercised while working, as well as the productivity that results from honest work, are both parts of God's blessing. Work, we must remember, is a gift from God that preceded Adam's sin. It is a blessing that existed in the garden of Eden prior to God's judgment on a fallen world. Work itself is a good thing. It is one of the Creator's first gifts to the people made in His image. It is "very good," as God Himself said, after putting the first couple to work (Gen. 1:31).

I know it is tempting at the dinner table to decompress from a tough day at work with a lot of talk about the hassles and problems at the office, but as good coaches we must never leave the wrong impression about the value God places on His creatures' engagement in their daily work. We need to make sure our boys hear the upside of a productive day on the job. They need to know that Mom and Dad recognize and even celebrate the value and privilege of reflecting God's design for His people by engaging daily in industrious employment. Purpose to speak well of your work. Discuss your work the way you hope your boy will be discussing his work twenty years from now.

When you speak of the future with your boys be sure to imagine their *possible* occupations, not that "dream job" or the you-can-do-anything-you-desire fantasies that our world is so accustomed to. Speak about the value of an honest day's work. Be mindful of how many twenty-somethings are stuck in an endless unemployed holding pattern, chasing the mirage of a perfectly fulfilling and super-high-paying career. The Bible says this is foolish. It is like running after some completely gratifying, get-rich-quick opportunity (Prov. 12:11; 28:19–20). Your son's future willingness to be a diligent, God-glorifying worker begins by your discussions with him that refuse to inflate his sense of entitlement. It starts by envisioning with him a future of feeling content about coming home tired from a good day's work, regardless of how glitzy or exciting his job may or may not be. It begins by speaking often of how God made us to bring Him honor by strategizing and working for the good of our own families and the common good of our own communities.

ABOUT CHORES

Adults have jobs, and kids have chores. Chores, like jobs, are aimed at the common good. They are tasks from which some positive benefit is derived for the family. They are assignments through which our children learn that their efforts produce advantages for everyone. And if you are thinking that your boy is too young to have chores, remember that even a one-year-old can engage in tasks that assist you throughout the day. Your boy can hand you things that you need. If they can walk, they can bring something helpful to you, or take something to your spouse that he or she needs. They need to be enlisted to help often, and be frequently praised for the way their effort was helpful.

By the time our boys were four or five years old, we had developed a household chore chart. We bought a twenty-eight-inch square pocket chart at the local teacher's supply store. We then took happy pictures of our boys engaged in the tasks we expected them to accomplish every day and had them laminated. There were smiling pictures of our boys engaged in daily chores, which were for their own benefit like brushing their teeth, putting on their shoes, "reading" the Bible (which consisted of looking through their Bible picture book), and praying. There were also happy pictures of them busy with tasks that benefited the family, like setting the table, putting dirty cups in the sink, and cleaning up the family room by putting toys away in the toy box. The chart had columns marked "not done" and "done." The chart hung low on a wall in the kitchen, where they could reach out each day and move the picture of a chore from the "not done" column to the "done" column.

The chore chart was a way for our boys to accept a sense of responsibility for a growing set of age-appropriate tasks that were for their good and the good of their family. They were able to feel a sense of accomplishment as they moved their pictures to the "done" column. It was a visual way for them to see at the end of each day that they had completed the good work that was expected of them. Every night after we put them to sleep, we'd reset the chore chart and start all over again the next day.

As our boys got older we retired the chore chart, but not the concept. They had an increasingly challenging list of weekly duties that we would expect needed to be tackled in any modern household—things like hauling the trash cans back and forth to the curb (which, until recently when my boys both left for college, I had all but forgotten how to do). When assigning the regular or special tasks to our boys, we often reminded them that "we are a family" and "when the family needs something, we are all going to pitch in to see the family needs met." Soon this was a common comeback from one child to another, *after* they had learned that it would get them nowhere to protest with the "Why do *I* have to do *that*?" Our goal was to teach them from the beginning that your work is not only for you, your own benefit, but God has called us all to work for the good of others.

As I explained in chapter 2, this principle was underscored by the service we required of them in the ministries at our church, and by means of the service projects, hospital visitations, and missions trips we took them on and sent them on. From making their beds and cleaning their rooms, to working in poorer neighborhoods in our area and running vacation Bible school in various places, our hope was to instill the value of sacrificial hard work for the glory of God and the good of others.

ABOUT LAZINESS

A Christian work ethic stands in stark contrast to laziness. Our natural tendency may be to seek out all of life's comforts and conveniences whenever possible, but without a commitment to hard work, any experience of comfort or conveniences will be rare and eventually out of reach. The Bible consistently deplores a lethargic and inactive approach to life. God warns us of the fruit of being a slothful person. Consider just a few of the proverbs that speak to this issue:

Go to the ant, O sluggard; consider her ways, and be wise. Without having any chief, officer, or ruler, she prepares her bread in summer and gathers her food in harvest. How long will you lie there, O sluggard? When will you arise from your sleep? A little sleep, a little slumber, a little folding of the hands to rest, and poverty will come upon you like a robber, and want like an armed man. (Prov. 6:6–11)

A slack hand causes poverty, but the hand of the diligent makes rich. He who gathers in summer is a prudent son, but he who sleeps in harvest is a son who brings shame. (10:4–5)

The soul of the sluggard craves and gets nothing, while the soul of the diligent is richly supplied. (13:4)

In all toil there is profit, but mere talk tends only to poverty. (14:23)

Whoever is slack in his work is a brother to him who destroys. (18:9)

Whoever works his land will have plenty of bread, but he who follows worthless pursuits will have plenty of poverty. (28:19)

Knowing and genuinely believing these truths will go a long way in motivating us to help our boys root out the laziness that is built into their fallen nature. Like any changes we are trying to affect in our growing sons, we need to be nurturing and strategic. We don't want to exasperate or demoralize our boys by simply chiding them for their bent to value fun over toil. We can all sympathize with that. But we must see the danger of raising a man who despises hard work and is always looking for a way out of it. Knowing that the self-discipline of persevering in diligent and faithful work will always reap both tangible and intangible dividends, we must consistently highlight and value the benefits that come from our sons' labor.

Modeling is critical here. It is next to impossible to instill a positive attitude toward industrious work if our boys sense the hypocrisy of our words. A positive attitude toward productive labor and our dislike for laziness, idleness, and excessive hours in front of a television need to be demonstrated by Mom and Dad. A disdain for laziness is as much caught as taught. So let's take an objective look at our schedules and make sure we are setting a good example of conscientiously investing our time in pursuits, both professionally and as volunteers for the honor of Christ and the benefit of others.

MAKING EXCUSES

God tells us that excuse-making and laziness go hand in hand. If our son learns that a good excuse will relieve him of the burden of a task or a chore, he will become an expert at manufacturing them. Proverbs tells us the lazy person will come up with a clever excuse, "There is a lion outside!" (22:13), and think himself wise in doing so (26:16).

Whatever it takes for the slacker to talk his way out of his

111

responsibilities (and stay in bed, in the case of the sluggard of Proverbs 26:13–14), he will creatively come up with it. We may all be tempted to be excuse-makers, but if we are going to raise men, excuses in our home cannot be tolerated.

With that said, let us make sure we understand the nature of an excuse. Unlike explanations, excuses seek to relieve us of responsibility. An excuse is a conveniently crafted explanation that attempts to hide the real reasons that something did or did not happen, in hopes that the burden of the assignment will simply go away. The contents of an excuse may be partly true, but they seek to conceal the whole story, namely that the person wanted to get out of doing whatever it was they were supposed to do. That may be more of a definition than was needed, because (as experienced excuse-makers ourselves) we can usually detect an excuse when we hear one.

When you do hear an excuse, insist on the truth. The truth may be painful (e.g., "I was lazy and I didn't want to do it"), but the whole truth is what we need. Once again, to create a domestic culture where excuses are not allowed, we as parents will need to model clear and direct admissions when we fail to carry out our responsibilities. We need to resolve to never make excuses, and to be brief when we do provide explanations. "I am sorry. I should have done that," will be a better educational practice to model for our boys than trying to pull off the illusion that we never fail to do everything on our to-do list. Faithfulness? Yes! Perfect consistency? Impossible! Be faithful parents who refuse to make excuses.

RESTING TO WORK

With all this transparent talk of how we attempted to instill a good Christian work ethic in our boys, you might think that my wife and I were the "all-work-and-no-play" taskmaster parents. Well, that's just not true. We understood the value of rest, recreation, and fun. More than just the daily playtime mentioned in the previous chapter, there was a reasonable priority placed on family fun times. As a matter of fact, the scheduling of trips to the amusement park, the zoo, or the sporting event served an important role in seeking to instill a balanced Christian work ethic in my children.

Such balance should start with the common work-before-play principle. Most parents are quick to employ this when there are beds to make before a trip to the park, or when there are toys to pick up before dinner. But wise parents will take this one step further. The Bible warns us that it is easy to idolize rest and recreation. We are warned by God to "Love not sleep" and "eat only enough" of the sweet treat of honey lest you "vomit it" (Prov. 20:13; 25:16). When, as parents, we only hold out the promise of fun times as treats to be worked toward, we create in our sons the all-too-common "Wednesday hump day" and "Thank God it's Friday" mentality. If, as the old 80s song goes, "Everybody's working for the weekend," then we are bound to raise clock-watchers who will never approach their work "as to the Lord" (Col. 3:23).

To counter this, my wife and I regularly scheduled breaks, trips, and recreation as activities, which we clearly presented as ways to "re-create" our minds and bodies so that we could serve the Lord in our daily work. We wanted our boys to learn to love to engage in the work God called them to do. And we wanted them to see the role of taking an appropriate amount of fun and tranquil breaks to recharge, reorient, and regroup, so that they could reengage in the daily tasks they were made to tackle. "A tranquil heart gives life to the flesh," Proverbs 14:30 states. We need that life "recreated" in us through joyful times when we will "not do any ordinary work." I put those words in quotes because it is the phrase used in the Bible twelve times, as God scheduled Israel's annual calendar. They were told to participate in various feasts and festivals that were to be characterized by joy and celebration—events during which the people were to "not do any ordinary work." We have to schedule these for our kids—weekly and throughout the year. They will not be able to resist looking forward to these times as you schedule them, but be sure they are rightly understood as important breaks to refresh us for our daily tasks.

While many will go to work just so they can rest, let us raise young men who will be careful to consistently and adequately rest so that they can glorify God in their work.

THE IMPORTANCE OF SCHEDULES

Just as God scheduled an annual calendar for the ancient people of Israel with a perfect balance of work and re-creative rest, we need to help our boys from an early age keep strategically planned schedules. It starts with daily routines in which our young sons can learn to expect a well-balanced day of activities: mealtimes, chore times, nap times, story times, chill times, and activity times. The consistency of moms and dads faithfully maintaining these schedules can have a securing and healthy effect on the lives of our children.

Think of schedules as you would think of a financial budget. If you fail to have your son budget for it, he likely won't have any time left for it. Time, like money, gets spent on the things that are easy to "buy." Don't expect him to have any leftover time for cleaning his room. If the task is a priority to you, or should be for him, then it needs to be scheduled.

When our boys were young, we would post their schedules in a prominent place in the kitchen. As they grew older, we would post a schedule on the computer that we could all access, consult, and edit. We always remembered that we were masters of the calendar and not slaves to it. But we also recognized that a schedule could never be of any service to us if we didn't determine to keep it.

I am confident that as my boys look back on their childhoods filled with chores, homework, family dinners, sports, youth groups, service projects, music, Bible studies, park days, and vacations, they will re-member their time as a part of our schedule-keeping family, as busy but manageable, active but reasonable, and planned but productive. I pray that as they have learned the discipline of managing time, it will aid them in becoming faithful stewards of the lives God has entrusted to each of them.

INSTILLING A MANLY WORK ETHIC

Allow me again to bring this chapter in for a landing with some spiritual common sense that my wife and I have found helpful in instilling a biblical work ethic in our boys. It is my hope that these tips can help construct a positive sense of order, structure, and productivity that will pay off as your boy becomes a man.

Getting Up

Like most parents of active little boys, we rarely needed our boys up in the morning before they were naturally raring to go. The battle early on is to get those boys to sleep and to stay in bed until a reasonable hour. We as their parents always determined what that reasonable hour was, and we were determined to win the battle of them staying in bed until that hour. Even before our sons could read we made sure they understood how to decipher the numbers on their bedside clock. For instance, we would tell them, "Your day will start at seven o'clock, and that means you will stay in this bed, quietly resting until those numbers on that clock read 'Seven, zero, zero.'" Initially, we even wrote out the numbers on a three-by-five card and leaned it against the clock.

Having them learn the self-discipline of laying quietly in bed until 7:00 a.m. gave Mom and Dad the time to get up early and to work through our spiritual disciplines and other domestic duties before our boys were in the mix. If you set the standard and enforce any infractions early on, it is amazing how orderly your mornings can be, at least by comparison to your boys banging on your bedroom door at 5:00 a.m.

But What About . . .

BOYS SLEEPING LATE

Our little boys need to sleep in spite of their desire to get up early. But what about our tween and teen boys? For early to late adolescents, the problem typically is not waking too early. Often on school days they may not rouse at all! You or your spouse must go in their rooms to wake them because they did not hear the alarm—or they heard it, turned it off, and fell back to sleep.

This is a different problem caused by two situations. As growing teens, they need more sleep. But as teens they also may be distracted at bedtime by cellphones that offer texting, social media, even videos, and you may be unaware of it. Studies show that the small-lit screens of smartphones stimulate the mind; after turning off his phone your teen needs up to thirty minutes to fall asleep. Even if the distraction is "only" an extended phone call, it's keeping your son or daughter awake. The bedroom may be dark, but your child is active. So set house rules that mean when lights are out, phones are off. You may need to agree that phones depart the room at true bedtime.

Such rules will also help on Sunday mornings when your teen says he or she is too tired to get up for church. While you may permit your child to stay up a little later on Friday and Saturday nights, even those nights be sure that all distractions, especially cellphones and headphones, are off and off-limits when bedtime comes.

Nap Time

Daily nap time for our young boys (generally for those age five and under) was much like the morning interval between waking and getting up. They didn't need to sleep, but they did need to be quiet on their beds. We made it our habit not to tell them to "go to sleep," but rather to "take a break" and "get some down time." A child's nap time is an important window of opportunity for a busy mom to catch up on what she needs to accomplish—which at times means taking a quick power nap herself. Whatever Mom chooses to do, it is important that our sons learn the discipline and self-control to lay quietly on their own beds by themselves without any demands on their parents.

These periodic daily quiet times are an important contribution to their strength, energy, and ability to maintain a disposition that wasn't overly tired, spent, or cranky. These times need to be disciplined, even if as toddlers they don't sleep, but just sit silently on their beds flipping through their books or peacefully play with a toy. It is important to be consistent and scheduled about these times, so your sons can begin to experience the pattern of rest and "work" that aids their well-being.

The Egg Timer and the Checklist

A simple nine-dollar wind-up egg timer was one of the most frequently used tools in helping our young boys learn to keep and value a schedule. Whether it was reading time, break time, or challenging them to get their math homework done in twenty-five minutes, it seemed that trusty little egg timer was often ticking in our house. We kept it from being a taskmaster and encouraged them to see it as a game to try and "beat the buzzer" when it involved all their various tasks, chores, or projects.

You might be tempted to keep the countdown clock to yourself, by using the timer on your phone, but our goal wasn't simply to remember when to prompt them to move from one thing to the next. The goal was to train our young boys to experience the management of time and to learn the need for scheduling, by having that egg timer in their environment as they worked.

A great way for kids—and their parents—to be productive is to make a checklist and cross off items during the day. Crafting specific lists of things to do can help a young boy develop a sense of progress and accomplishment. The "chores" list was an example of this, but this simple tool can be used many other ways. Using daily, weekly, and even monthly lists for personal, spiritual, and educational tasks can make a huge difference in helping your children make progress in the various areas of their lives. As the saying goes: "If you aim at nothing, you'll hit it every time!" Let's cultivate a godly work ethic in our sons by utilizing reasonable to-do lists that give them a sense of triumph and achievement in the responsibilities that will stretch them and develop them as productive young men.

Homework

Homework will always be a struggle for fidgety boys. But the discipline to keep their rear ends in the chair will serve them well for the rest of their lives. You might tackle this daily hurdle after your sons have a quick opportunity after school to blow off some steam, whether in the driveway shooting baskets or in the backyard kicking the ball around. It can be a short time—just enough to let them sweat a little before they hit the books. In the early years you can help them prioritize their work for the afternoon by putting the most challenging assignments at the top of the list.

For us, Carlynn would set our trusty timer and tell them they would have a ten-minute break after working on the list for fifty minutes. When they were younger, say first through third grade, we'd make the work time twenty-five minutes before the ten-minute break. The breaks weren't for television or screen games. We had an ample arsenal of nerf balls, indoor hoops, nerf guns, soft-dart targets, their junior putters, and a small pile of golf balls. We wanted our boys up and around, throwing things, making baskets, or even wrestling with one another for ten minutes. Then it was back to the books until the list was done for the afternoon.

For the Fabarez boys, the end of homework for each day became official when they began to pack their backpacks for the next day of school, and then put those fabric bags by the door. Prioritized lists, timers, and breaks were helpful in getting them to that satisfying moment of zipping up their packed bag for tomorrow.

CHORES TO PREPARE FOR ADULTHOOD

Dinner

In our busy home, dinner together as a family could not take place every day, but we did work to make it a more-often-than-not reality. If homework was done, our boys were usually called in from outside activities early enough to wash up and help Mom with the last-minute preparation for our family dinner. They would set the table, grate the cheese, and pour the milk.

After dinner the boys were always expected to help clear the table, clean the kitchen, pack the leftovers, and do whatever else might be needed. As they were a part of the family, these nightly chores weren't seen as chores, just as a basic expectation of enjoying the benefits of a working kitchen. Encourage your children to participate, so they will learn household chores before they are out of the house. Not only will they learn an essential life skill early, but you will not inadvertently instill a sense of entitlement in your boys, that others are supposed to cater to their every craving.

Laundry

Before your boy leaves your home, you would do well to turn over to him all the responsibilities of sorting, washing, drying, folding, ironing, and perhaps mending his own clothes. At some point in high school, if not before, train your son to operate these automated machines that do so much of the work for us. Our great-great-grandparents would laugh at the modern parent's reluctance of turning over the task of washing and drying clothes in these "miracle machines" they knew nothing of.

Much like learning what goes into preparing a meal, it is important for our boys to learn that their clothes don't magically mutate from a disheveled pile in the hamper to a neatly folded stack in their dressers. Teach them how to sew on a button, stitch up a tear, scrub out a grass stain, and to put the right amount of detergent in the washing machine. Unless you're sending a butler with them to college, they will be confronted with the challenge eventually. Teach them ahead of time, and allow them the unspoken gratification of taking care of their own clothes.

Crawl In, Don't Call In

We all know what it is like to work through a cold, or to have to endure a cough at a meeting as we labor to meet a deadline at work. If every sniffle our boys have is an acceptable excuse to miss church, stay home from school, or miss a game, then we will never teach them the life skill of working through slight physical discomforts. This is a major part of raising men, not boys. We are preparing them to be adults.

Certainly I am not including those days our boys are running a fever or infected with a contagious illness, but every parent should soon learn that the variety of tummy aches and "I-don't-feel-that-good" mornings aren't always significant impediments. Our sons need to be taught that life's minor aches and pains most often need to be set aside in light of a day's tasks.

Expect your boys to test and retest you on this. They want to know how soft you will be on letting them off the hook when they are facing something difficult, unpleasant, or nerve-racking. It may be overstated to say a good worker "crawls in" instead of "calls in," but some days it feels that way for all of us. Teach them this important aspect of a manly work ethic by encouraging them to power through the minor discomforts of everyday life.

7

HELP HIM FOSTER DOMINION OVER HIS WALLET

Money. What a hassle!

In the grown-up world of mortgages, income tax, auto repairs, and medical insurance premiums, it doesn't take much experience to have a visceral reaction of frustration to the topic of personal finances. With so much stress and irritation associated with household budgets, monthly bills, and our need to store up an adequate savings for the future, most parents choose to shield their young children from this frustrating part of life.

But we shouldn't; at least, not completely. As responsible Christian parents, we must prepare our young boys to be faithful and trustworthy managers of the material blessings God will entrust to them when they are paying mortgages and saving for our grandchildren's college tuition.

FOR THE LOVE OF MONEY

Before we attempt to impart our parental instruction concerning money to our boys, we'd better step back and make sure we align our thoughts with God's timeless wisdom on this volatile topic. And that's a good place to start—with one of the most familiar Bible verses on money that speaks of its explosive effects: "For the love of money is a root of all kinds of evils. It is through this craving that some have wandered away from the faith and pierced themselves with many pangs" (1 Tim. 6:10).

We certainly don't want these injurious effects in the life of our child! So, knowing that the Bible is clear that our boy's relationship with money has the potential of derailing his spiritual interests and development, we had better begin early to educate him as to how God would have him interface with this inescapable part of life.

Notice, by the way, that this verse is often misquoted. It does not say that "money is the root of all kinds of evil" but that "the *love* of money is the root of all kinds of evil." That is a big difference. We cannot escape a life of interacting with money, and many godly men will do so for their entire lives with exemplary hearts. The problem comes when men begin to love, crave, and chase after money as though it has a power that it does not have.

The Lie about Money

It seems that everyone, especially our young and inexperienced sons, are susceptible to the lie that more money will grant us what we really crave. It is a deception that some people never outgrow. Yes, more money spent on a car will get you a nicer car. No argument there. More money dumped into a house will get you a nicer house with multiplied comforts and conveniences. That is true. But we have to listen to God's wisdom, along with the testimony of countless people who have insisted that nicer things and an increase in comforts and conveniences don't grant what we presumed they would.

Being made in the image of God, all people have sincere needs for things that God is able to supply through a variety of means that don't require a big bank account. We naturally crave joy, security, and significance, which are all part of our nature as creatures made for relationships—especially a foundational relationship with our Creator that's free from controlling sin and guilt. These fundamental cravings cannot be achieved through a purchase at the auto mall or the real estate office. That is why the Bible reminds us of what we've all heard countless times but decide to ignore. Consider the richest king of the Old Testament:

I said in my heart, "Come now, I will test you with pleasure; enjoy yourself." But behold, this also was vanity. I said of laughter, "It is mad," and of pleasure, "What use is it?". . . . I built houses and planted vineyards for myself. I made myself gardens and parks, and planted in them all kinds of fruit trees. I made myself pools from which to water the forest of growing trees. I bought male and female slaves, and had slaves who were born in my house. I had also great possessions of herds and flocks, more than any who had been before me in Jerusalem. I also gathered for myself silver and gold and the treasure of kings and provinces. . . .

And whatever my eyes desired I did not keep from them. I kept my heart from no pleasure, for my heart found pleasure in all my toil, and this was my reward for all my toil. Then I considered all that my hands had done and the toil I had expended in doing it, and behold, all was vanity and a striving after wind, and there was nothing to be gained under the sun. (Eccl. 2:1–11)

I know what you're thinking. It is what I think every time someone gives a testimony about reaching the top, having it all—the sports cars, the lucrative contracts, the mammoth houses, the private jet—and then says, "None of it made me happy!" I think: "Let me give it a try; I think I might just be able to be happy with all of that stuff."

But watch the TV specials on the curse of Lotto winners or read the stories of ex-sports stars, or the biographies of the guy who had everything, and at some point we recognize the cumulative evidence of human beings who are honest enough to say that bigger and better purchases didn't make for better marriages, more fulfilling jobs, or more satisfying relationships with God.

You and I—as well as our boys—don't have to try it. It is a mirage. Having some money is better than having no money, sure, but Christians, of all people, ought to be able to say with the apostle Paul that we have learned "the secret of facing plenty and hunger, abundance and need" because we know the big lie concerning money and the incomparable value of right relationships—starting with God Himself (see Phil. 4:11–13).

Achieving this kind of contentment through a godly pursuit of knowing Christ and rightly relating to those God puts in our lives should replace the hopeless pursuit of being happy by amassing more money and the things it can buy. This is the logic that precedes the familiar verse about the "love of money" in the passage we first looked at.

> But godliness with contentment is great gain, for we brought nothing into the world, and we cannot take anything out of the world. But if we have food and clothing, with these we will be content. But those who desire to be rich fall into temptation, into a snare, into many senseless and harmful desires that plunge people into ruin and destruction. (1 Tim. 6:6–9)

Jesus said, "One's life does not consist in the abundance of his possessions" (Luke 12:15). It is time we prove that we believe this truth by the way we instruct our boys and live out our values before them every day.

Generosity or Greed?

From the beginning, God wants the household in which your boy is raised to be characterized by generosity instead of greed. Does your boy live in a home where he witnesses the relative unimportance of money over and against relationships? Or does your boy, like so many, live in a home that declares money is unimportant, while his parents crave and chase more of it? In other words, do you prize wealth by what you celebrate, what you argue about, and what you prioritize? Scripture declares, "He who loves money will not be satisfied with money, nor he who loves wealth with his income" (Eccl. 5:10). It is an addiction of sorts. It would be like telling your kids all weekend about the harm of smoking, but then spending all week with the jitters in pursuit of your next cigarette.

The problem with that illustration is, unlike the smoker addicted to nicotine who can remove himself from it with various treatments (or going through "cold turkey" withdrawals), we cannot rid ourselves of money, an essential of commerce and often survival. But there is a way to break our penchant to crave money. Note God's counsel from our passage in 1 Timothy:

> As for the rich in this present age, charge them not to be haughty, nor to set their hopes on the uncertainty of riches, but on God, who richly provides us with everything to enjoy. They are to do good, to be rich in good works, to be generous and ready to share, thus storing up treasure for themselves as a good foundation for the future, so that they may take hold of that which is truly life. (6:17–19)

The instructions are not to remove all money from your environment and give up the good-paying job. No, the biblical exhortation is to prove your lack of addiction to this volatile commodity. It is a call to exercise humility, to trust in God to provide what is necessary. As we set our hopes "on God, who richly provides us with everything to enjoy", we can engage in a regular pattern of doing good, which will include a lot of generous acts of giving and sharing. This, we are told, is an indispensable component of what is described as "truly life"—the thing that money cannot buy.

SHARING

Do you want to teach your boys to be generous with their money? If so, you must first teach them how to share. Sharing our possessions is an expression of our lack of addiction to the things that money can buy. To be ready to share is to be willing, eager, and committed to the practice of letting other people enjoy the things our money has purchased.

Every parent intuitively senses the ugliness of a child who selfishly clutches his toys and refuses to share them. Parents naturally see the "right" in having their boys share—especially when other parents are standing around watching! This awkward moment has played out countless times and reminds us that if we can't teach our boys to share at home, they will certainly not do it at the church nursery or the school playground, and likely not as a pattern in their adult life.

Teaching our boys to share will, of course, require us to step up in those moments when we have to pry things out of their hands and deal with the whining that follows. But the pattern of experiencing something of that "true life" the Bible talks about when we are ready to share, must be caught in our households and not just taught when our friends' kids are over at our home. We must show our boys by our example that we are willing, eager, and committed to letting others experience the benefits of the things we have purchased.

Do you have people over to your home as a regular practice? It obviously is not without cost, inconvenience, and some level of pressure, but it is an expression of the biblical virtue of hospitality that your boys will either experience and learn from you, or will be something foreign to them and absent from their childhood. Let your boys see your grace and generosity in willingly preparing for guests, warmly receiving them, and patiently forgiving them when their coffee is spilled on your carpet. This will speak volumes about your value of people above stuff. You will model for them the essence of the Christlike attribute of loving

But What About . . .

TEACHING HOSPITALITY

What about your children as they watch you entertain guests at home? Let them practice hospitality with you. From the earliest possible age, enlist your sons and daughters to help you set up your home, put out the snacks, light the candles, vacuum the floor, set the table, and greet your guests at the door.

Give them instructions ahead of time as to how to serve both your guests and your guest's children while they are in your home. Get them to think through how they can involve the other children in games, engage in eye-to-eye conversations with the adults, and come up with ways that no child is left out of the events and activities that will take place.

If there are no other children at your house on a particular night, be sure you have clearly talked through their bedtime, and how their sacrificial gift to your guests is their obedience to go to bed without objection and complaint.

When your boys are old enough to be up when your guests leave, make sure they join in with your non-complaining, joyful, willing engagement in cleaning up. Reminisce with them about the night, as you reassemble the house and clean the kitchen.

people instead of the stuff your paycheck can purchase. And they can practice hospitality with you. (See "But What About" sidebar.)

Your home is the most all-encompassing way to model your priority of people over stuff, but it may not be the most impressionable to your boys. For example, your willingness to share your vehicle with a family at the church who needs it might leave a lasting lesson for your son. A costly gift, presented with joy to a next-door neighbor going through a difficult season of life, might be recalled by your sons as a virtue to be mimicked decades later. Think practically, and seek to model for your boys a daily pattern of lending, generosity, and the holding of the things of the world loosely for the sake of Christ.

GIVING TO THE CHURCH

My second-born son, John, was about five when I told him to collect what he had in the "giving jar" on his dresser, so that he could put it in the offering at church on the forthcoming Sunday. (See more on "the giving jar" on page 135). Perplexed, he looked at me and said, "But I thought we were going to give that money to God." I smiled and asked, "How do you suggest we do that?" He shrugged.

John, of course, had the right intention about giving to God, but he was ignorant about the agency of our giving. On the other hand, far too many grown-up Christians are mistakenly focused on the intermediary role of the church budget, and have missed the biblical intention of giving our material resources as an act of worship to God.

As parents, we want our children to make sure the focus stays on the ultimate Recipient of our gifts, with an intelligent appreciation of the church that receives our gifts on His behalf. As in the Old Testament, where the daily sacrifices and offerings of the farming Israelites supplied the operating needs of the worship center and the meals for the Levitical priests, our financial gifts to God are combined to pay the church electric bill, the employee health insurance premiums, and maintaining every fixture and piece of furniture in the building. We should help our boys understand this important arrangement God has ordained, without having them lose the sacred nature of the money they bring to give in the weekly offering.

Your son's act of financially giving to the Lord is sacred and important, not only because God has commanded that we give gifts to Him (Prov. 3:9), but also because it is an exercise in remembering that our Creator and Sustainer is the Giver of *all* that your son has or ever will receive. We must teach them early the utter dependence we all inherently have on the Lord's moment-by-moment provision in our lives. This may not be a challenge when they are young, as they take money from your hand to directly deposit it in the offering plate, but if they haven't learned this lesson early, by the time they are in high school working at the fast-food place down the street, they will begin to foolishly imagine that the paycheck they earn, they earned on their own. God was quick to correct this thinking way back in the fifth book of the Bible: "Beware lest you say in your heart, 'My power and the might of my hand have gotten me this wealth.' You shall remember the LORD your God, for it is he who gives you power to get wealth" (Deut. 8:17–18a).

Were it not for God's generous provision of life, health, and a properly functioning mind, the most industrious worker would be incapable of earning a dime. Our boys must learn to express this foundational understanding of God's active involvement in His creation by learning to give to God—consistently participating in the worship of giving at church.

While the New Testament doesn't re-legislate the various tithes that were required of the Israelites (yes, there were more than one), a tithe, which means "tenth," isn't a bad place to start with our boys. We always encouraged more than 10 percent, reminding our boys that "God loves a cheerful giver" (2 Cor. 9:7). Just by instilling the simple thought that God loves our generosity, my kids were quick to give as much as 50 percent of their allowance to God. This openhandedness was challenged in their young hearts as they grew and were saving up for this or that big purchase, but the practice of giving big certainly established a pattern that developed lasting habits.

When giving becomes difficult for them, remind your boys that they should never say they cannot afford to give. The reality is that they can't afford not to! God's disposition toward his generous creatures is no different than your disposition toward your son when he is generous. The morning I observe my son being stingy and tightfisted with his toys, my response to his requests at the department store that afternoon is not so big-hearted. If, on the other hand, I see my son sharing and being sacrificial with his toys, my response to his wishes at the mall that day will likely be much more benevolent. This is also the reasonable reaction of our Creator and will apply throughout your boy's life. Scripture says: "One gives freely, yet grows all the richer; another withholds what he should give, and only suffers want. Whoever brings blessing will be enriched, and one who waters will himself be watered" (Prov. 11:24–25).

ALLOWANCE

It would be unwise to wait until our sons have after-school jobs for them to feel the biblical sense of sacrifice when they give. This is one of the primary reasons I established my boys' allowance as early as they had an awareness that money is important and can procure for them a variety of the things they wanted. Of course, as parents we will purchase the things our children need (and then some!), but I wanted my boys to have the management of a small amount of money on a weekly basis so that they would experience a taste of its purchasing power, in concert with the call to give a portion of it away! This is when giving to God and others starts to mean something—when it is felt.

I have heard some parents say, "I don't want to give my kids an allowance for doing chores that come with just being a part of the family." I understand that sentiment, but my motive in introducing an allowance to my young children is less about the relationship between wages and work, and more about the opportunity for the training and guidance I can give them in learning how to give away a generous portion of what they value. With that said, I should be clear that once my boys discovered they could buy a candy bar or a small toy with their own money, they were excited and began to understand the value of money. I gladly controlled that small stream of income to develop both their faithfulness in handling money and learning the godly work ethic we looked at in the last chapter. And, of course, I reminded them to give a portion of their allowance to the Lord through the church.

SAVING

God has always advised prudence in our savings. He advises us to consider the ant that "prepares her bread in summer and gathers her food in harvest" (Prov. 6:8). We are told "wealth gained hastily will dwindle, but whoever gathers little by little will increase it" (13:11). The biblical virtue of saving, though, should never be used as a cover for hoarding. This is a delicate balance for Christians. We must instill in our boys that saving is important and necessary, but it cannot be used as an excuse for not giving faithfully to God or to others when they are in need.

From the time you begin to give your son an allowance, be sure to insist on saving for the future. This is not the kind of short-term saving for a game or a skateboard. I am talking about the kind of savings that won't be accessed for several years. I opened savings accounts for my boys at my bank, and from the time they were in grade school I would remind them about their need to buy a used car when they got their driver's license, and about that expensive thing called an engagement ring, which they would need to buy when they wanted to get married one day. When grandparents and other relatives started to give cash for birthdays or Christmas, I would remind them of their long-term needs, and many times they would choose to save all but ten or fifteen percent, which they would give to God.

You may want to match this long-term savings each time they made a deposit, at least during their first few years. I did this and found it easy when they were stashing away ten or twenty bucks. It got harder for me on those Christmases or birthdays when their grandparents went crazy with the cash gifts. But they saved and I chose to match their deposits until their sixteenth birthdays. And I am relieved to report that my sons had faithfully saved enough over the years (with my matching support) for both of them to purchase used cars, with cash, by the time they got their driver's licenses! Even with that big purchase they still had a modest balance to build on for that next big purchase.

GETTING PRACTICAL

Let me wrap this up with some practical steps to helping your son learn to exercise dominion over his wallet.

Weekly Allowance

It would be hard for me to suggest an amount for you to budget for your son's allowance. That would depend on when and where you live and the economic realities of your family. I will say that the amount needs to increase with the age of your son. It should begin, as I wrote earlier, when your boy understands that money can be used to acquire things he sees at the checkout stand or in the toy section of the grocery store. Start then, and keep bumping it up periodically so that the habit of giving and saving is felt. In other words, make sure it is enough to experience the sacrifice of giving away and stashing away money they would naturally want to spend on things they would truly enjoy now.

The Giving Jar

My wife and I decorated plastic tumblers that sat prominently on each of our son's dressers and were marked "Money for God." As soon as they received their allowance, the first stop was to walk over to their dresser and put a portion of that money into the "Money for God" jar. This is the principle of giving off of the top, or "the first fruits" as the Bible put it for that agrarian culture. When the harvest came in, the very first portion of the crop was to be given over to the Lord. If a portion of the money your boy receives doesn't physically and immediately go into the giving jar, you may inadvertently teach your son to give God his leftovers. Don't. We would always let them choose the amount to put in this jar, as long as it was over ten percent.

I would have them clean out this jar periodically (ever month or so), put the money in an envelope, and take it to church. If your son's Sunday school or Junior Church program takes an offering (which I recommend it does), have them put their envelope in the offering plate, bag, or box. If not, have them give it to God in the main service, or give it to you to put in the offering for them.

The Saving Jar

Sitting next to the giving jar on their dressers was a matching plastic tumbler marked "Money for Savings." This was the second assignment after getting their small stack of ones. They could choose to put whatever they wanted in this jar. (They were quick to remind each other that this was the amount Dad would match.) I can even remember that one of them had etched the words "Dad Matches!" under the words "Money for Savings." Ha. It was cute before it hurt. But their young prudence added up and paid off for them.

Every month or so I would have them clean out their savings jar and give me the cash and coins so that I could do the math on what I needed to transfer to their online savings accounts. We would then flatten out the crumpled bills and recycle them as a portion of their weekly allowance.

Wallets and Banking

Here are two approaches I have found useful. Buy each child a wallet and later open a bank account for each. When my boys were in elementary school, I bought them wallets in which they kept their "operating cash." When they reached their teenage years, I discovered an online banking site that allowed them access to a specialty account; this gave them their first experience with online banking. It was limited, but helpful for them to receive their allowance from me online and to have the ability to spend with a debit card. This account was unrelated to the savings account, which I kept for them as an associated account in my bank. They could not access those funds, which we agreed were to be tucked away for used cars and small diamonds.

By their high school days, I found a bank that had nationwide access; I figured this would serve them well into college. It was a special "student account" with several limitations and full visibility and spending alerts that were sent to me. When they went off to college, these accounts were converted to regular checking accounts, into which their part-time employers could directly deposit their paychecks.

Gift Giving

There are many childhood settings wherein your son will be (or should be) expected to give a gift—Mother's Day, friends' birthday parties, Christmas, etc. Up until nine or ten years old, your boy can likely get away with giving his original artwork and various crafts, but eventually gifts that cost money are the norm.

Many parents simply buy presents for their son to give to his friends or family members. I, though, recommend you have him spend at least a portion of his own money for these gifts. A gift given that costs him nothing will hardly build generous character in your boy. So even if all the other parents underwrite the gifts their kids bring to the birthday party, make him put up a couple of his dollars. And knowing that your son's budget would only yield an embarrassingly small gift by comparison, supplement the rest as he picks out a gift for his friend.

RAISING MEN IN A WORLD HALF-FULL OF WOMEN

You already know it: sex sells. And sex is what the world will be selling your sons their entire lives. Unless you are living with your head in the sand, I shouldn't need to quote the overwhelming statistics about the sex-saturated culture in which we live.

Even if I were to chronicle the tens of thousands of sexually charged advertisements, allusions in media, and messaging that will bombard your child each year, my alarming statistics would be out of date by the time this book gets into your hands. What the so-called "sexual revolution" ushered into our Western culture during the 1960s has unleashed a torrent of hormone-laden enticements in which you and I are called to raise our sons. And it is getting worse.

But don't despair. Don't throw up your hands and think it is impossible to raise godly young men in a world like ours. Don't let the naïve convince you that the Bible is of no help because its instruction is hopelessly out of touch with the temptations your boy's generation faces. No, the Book that God delivered to us was not penned in a puritanical cultural context or against the backdrop of a blushing Victorian society. Not in the least! Much of the historical timespan in which God chose to inscribe His saving truth and His practical instructions was marked by such unbridled sexual norms that many of those "Bible time" generations would be envious of the restraints that still remain in our day.

That, of course, is not to say we shouldn't be vigilant and prepared; it's just to make clear that when God speaks to issues of personal holiness and sexual purity, we can be sure that even if our cultural ghetto becomes as promiscuous and unprincipled as Sodom and Gomorrah, the Lord knows how to rescue the godly from temptations. In fact, the Bible specifically declares that in 2 Peter 2:6–9. It won't be easy, but we can have hope, knowing the challenge is nothing new for those seeking to raise godly boys.

GUARDING VERSUS VILIFYING

Because of the way this in-your-face promiscuity and all of the sexual enticement has ramped up from the time we were kids, it is understandable that some parents have taken the approach of "protecting" their boys by trying to denigrate and badmouth the whole topic of sex. "If we can get them to think badly of girls and sex, and joke about them getting married when they are forty," they foolishly reason, "then they will stay out of the minefield of sexual sin." But this all-too-common approach is wrong and unbiblical. Furthermore, this approach will either simply fail because of their forthcoming hormonal tsunami, or worse, it will drive them underground, away from any conversation or counsel from you, and into a secret and hidden world of perversion and deviance.

We can learn something as parents from the strong warnings

against sexual sin penned to "sons" in the book of Proverbs. This biblical book is situated two doors down from the open celebration of weddings and marital sex in the Song of Solomon. Clearly the God-breathed wisdom of Solomon sought to guard the next generation of young men from pursuing selfish sexual indulgence with prostitutes, without vilifying the powerful and gratifying gifts of romance, marriage, and sex.

So if you find that you haven't spoken well of marriage and romance lately to your son, then perhaps you've fallen into the trap of trying to write off the whole topic of sexual desires in an effort to keep him out of the backseat of a car with his girlfriend. That is a losing strategy! Talk is important—both about the truth of what's going on (or will soon be going on) in his head, heart, and bloodstream, as well as stern warnings *and* positive conversations about the rewarding experience of marital love and romance.

By the way, the strategy of vilifying sex may seem like it works a lot better when it comes to your daughters, but it only "works" as a short-term prevention that sadly carries with it some disastrous long-term side effects that you wouldn't want to reside in your future daughter-in-law. But that, I suppose, is a discussion for another book!

THE POWER OF SEXUAL DESIRE

Long before your son feels sexual desires, our culture will throw images, ads, billboards, and storylines his way as though he already does. The glitzy and glossy presentation of the "food" of sex will be shoved in his face years before he has an appetite for it. Even with the best parental protections, there will be plenty that he encounters that, at some point, will need explanation from you. Count on it, and plan to put these presentations of sexual material in context for him. Have the discussion when he becomes inquisitive about the matter, or when the encounter is so in-your-face that you both can't avoid saying something about what you just saw or heard. I am not talking about the dreaded "sex talk," which most parents don't want to deal with (more on that shortly). I am talking about the simple clarification that puts the sexually charged image or statement that crinkled his eyebrow into the context of male/ female attraction and marriage. It was my practice, in those awkward moments, to succinctly declare to my prepubescent boys that these "weird things" were designed by God for Christians to enjoy when they are married. I would also be careful to tell my sons that sadly far too many people in this world think these kinds of things can be done whenever and with whomever they want. And lastly, I would always make clear that this "whenever/whomever approach" angers God, frustrates people, and always causes damage to people's relationships.

A brief commentary from Mom or Dad that affirms the good of sex in its proper context, along with a warning of the harm of sex out of context, is always better than trying to ignore the un-ignorable. Early on in his life your son may ignore it, and surprisingly it may not even raise an eyebrow, but realize that at some point even the little kid with no appetite or experience of "having a meal," will start to wonder about all the hype in "the food court at the mall."

Maybe that's a good analogy to utilize as we fast-forward the development of your son, and arrive at the place in time where God has not only flipped on the hormone switch so that he has an appetite, but you start to realize that he seems to be starving to death. Perhaps you've noticed him double, triple, and then quadruple-take on the teenage girl in the parking lot. Maybe you've observed his eyes pop out of his head as he locks on to the scantily clad starlet on the cover of the gossip rag at the grocery store check-out stand. It should be at that moment you realize you are raising your very "hungry" son in the food court of life. And not only are there the sights, sounds, and smells of every conceivable kind of delicious food, but there are also well-lit glossy photos of the best-selling plates everywhere!

I think dads reading this chapter understand all of that. Moms, it's to you that I need to emphasize the important battle that ensues in your son when he hits puberty. Your husband likely hasn't been all that transparent about the mental torture he endured when he was a junior higher. Even if he successfully avoided sexual activity through his teen years, you can be sure that he is able to better empathize with the painful internal battle that pubescent boys of any generation have to endure. You must not be shocked by the presence of these powerful pangs of interest that are part-and-parcel of boys with surging hormones, any more than your husband should be shocked if you missed lunch and decided to walk through a mall food court at six o'clock to grab a bite.

The presence of the interest in girls and your son's budding sexual desires are not the problem, nor are they abnormal, sinful, or shameful. The challenge for parents is to help our boys learn to exercise self-control—and such self-control *is* attainable. Not only do we not buy the culture's pessimistic lie that says: "Get real, they're *all* going to do it!", but we also cannot follow our generation's insistence that marriage (which is the sanctioned and godly context for sexual gratification) needs to be unrealistically postponed until your boy has hit all the worldly and materialistic benchmarks of adulthood. If we follow the world's cues by demanding from our boys the culture's prerequisites to marriage (i.e., degrees, down payments, international travel, etc.), we will risk demoralizing and exasperating them. We will unwittingly make obedience to God's commands extremely and profoundly difficult! Are you really willing to compound the risk of your son being disobedient to God's command to keep sexual activity inside the covenant of marriage, for the sake of satisfying the conventional expectations of your non-Christian neighbors and worldly relatives? I would hope not.

Be compassionate toward your son by positively recognizing God's endorsed and blessed context for marital love and sexual fulfillment. Be kind in acknowledging your support of his desire to identify and covenant with the biblically praised "wife of his youth" (Prov. 5:18, et al.) instead of toeing the line with our culture's expectation of him as a successful executive, walking the aisle with the "bride of his midlife." Of course this approach will require more of your parental prayers, counsel, planning, discipleship, and practical involvement. It will also require a recasting of what can be a positive image of a young couple struggling through the early years on a very tight budget. At the same time, you can be sure you are providing a much more hopeful, optimistic, and attainable perspective on this very important aspect of your son's life.

THE SEX TALK

After a series of your honest commentaries in response to the in-your-face sexual material your young son encounters, there still remains a need for that much-feared discussion about the birds and the bees. Don't put it off for too long. Remember that no matter how well you think you have insulated his childhood, he has been hearing and seeing sexual references and themes for years. And before you dismissively say, "My son doesn't know anything about that!", realize he is probably playing dumb with you and pretending to be informed with his friends. By the time your son feels awkward about being naked in the presence of others in his home, you can be sure that the intuitive and universally human sense of the uniqueness of his "private parts" has dawned on him to some degree. Clear, reasoned, biblically based, and age-appropriate answers will need to be provided by you about those "private parts," and how they correlate to who God has designed him to be as a sexual being.

Considering that the onset of puberty can be as early as nine or ten, and that exposure to sexual references is so pervasive in our society, you should purpose to get to "talking" sooner rather than later. If you procrastinate, you will by omission be handing your son's sex education over to a set of ill-informed and unfit peers. So start early. It won't be a one-time conversation. You'll likely need to revisit "the talk" a few times throughout your boy's elementary school years. But plan to have that initial conversation during his primary years. It may feel awkward, but it will at some level be a welcomed clarification from your boy's most trusted source of information.

Speaking of a "trusted source," while Mom may win that designation during your son's early years, this "talk" is best had with Dad, if possible. If your home is intact, and Dad is a part of your boy's everyday life, it is best for fathers to open up this topic of conversation with their sons. I can assure you, dads, that if "the talk" is had early, left with a proverbial open door, and followed up with periodic installments throughout the prepubescent years, your teen son will come back to you during his embattled teen years seeking your help, support, and encouragement about this catalytic part of his life. Dads, I know this can be a frightening assignment, but I exhort you to man up, work through your apprehensions, and have the discussion.

While several Christian books and Christian organizations have recommended a variety of details as to the kinds of things one would be wise to address during these early "talks,"[1] let me simply itemize a few essentials. Beyond the age-appropriate explanation of our human reproductive "plumbing," be sure to emphasize the following:

1. *The Special Value God Places on Sexuality*. Inform your son that sex is a very powerful and important aspect of our humanity on which God has placed a special value. God has a lot to say about sex in the Bible and He wants it to be enjoyed according to His instructions. As with all powerful things, it makes sense that sex is given to mankind with a set of warning labels that are spelled out in God's Word. These are important rules, and as a Christian family you are committed to being careful to abide by the Creator's directions about anything related to sex.

2. *God's Proper Context for Sexuality.* Tell your boy that sexual activity is a gift God has designed to be enjoyed between a man and a woman in the context of marriage. It is a loving activity that emotionally bonds a husband and wife together and also, in some cases (as you have explained), creates new life. God is so wise in giving this powerful expression of love and relationship to husbands and wives, and so you may tell your young son, "As weird as it may sound, when you get married you will be thankful for this gift from God."

3. *The Importance of Modesty.* Let your son know that because of the special value God places on human sexuality, He calls us to place a special value and modesty on our sexual organs. That is why we cover them up and consider them private. They are to be shared only in the relationship of marriage. That is why as a Christian family you don't make jokes about them, let other people see them, or try to look at anyone else's.

4. *The Problem with Our World.* Impress upon your son that most of the world is very rebellious as it relates to sexual issues. Way too many in our world have disregarded God's warnings and decided to experience sexual activities outside of the relationship of marriage. This always damages their relationships with people, and especially with God. Sadly, many are showing their private parts to each other in pictures or even in person, and displeasing God by trying to look at each other's sexual parts when they are not married to each other.

5. *A Willingness to Answer Questions.* During your "talks," invite your boy to ask you any questions he might have about his body, the topic of sex, marriage, or anything he has heard about boys and girls that has confused him. If he opens up, his questions

probably will take you back to your childhood curiosities and confusions. Answer his questions matter-of-factly, and warn him that you will likely need to talk about this subject again with him in the future. Tell him you realize this topic can be embarrassing, but reassure him that you want to be his reliable and godly source of information about this part of life.

CHIVALRY IS NOT DEAD

Sex and reproduction will obviously end up being a very small percentage of your son's lifetime of interacting with the opposite sex. Living in a world half-full of women will require a set of skills that needs to be imparted to him as sincerely and prayerfully as your discipleship, to ensure the fulfillment of sex in its sanctioned context, and the avoidance of the damage of sexual sin. You must work to instruct him early and regularly in the special challenge and privilege of interfacing with girls, young ladies, and women. Not only will this lay an appropriate foundation for a harmonious marriage, but it will also enable him to please God by living out the Lord's excellent and wise theology of gender.

It is essential that we remember that the Creator designed humanity in His own image. That image, of course, has nothing to do with the physical features of our bodies—for God is spirit and has no body! Rather it clearly refers to the divine reflection of personhood in our human spirit. Genesis 1:27 informs us that this divine reflection is not bound up exclusively in the personal characteristics of masculinity, but it is also seen in the personal characteristics of femininity: "So God created man in his own image, in the image of God he created him; male and female he created them (Gen. 1:27).

This simple yet profound statement of Scripture is the opening proposition relating to the biblical doctrine known as *complementarianism*. That is a fancy way of expressing the appreciation and respect that each gender should hold and express toward the distinctiveness of the other. Men and women have distinct outlooks, and in marriage they complement—and complete—each other. As it is put in the New Testament, "In the Lord woman is not independent of man nor man of woman; for as woman was made from man, so man is now born of woman. And all things are from God" (1 Cor. 11:11–12).

From the beginning, we need to instill in our boys the practice of honor, courtesy, and respect for the opposite sex. God's creative design is esteemed, and God Himself is glorified when our boys can sincerely affirm that girls are not "icky and gross," they don't have cooties, and boys are not in competition with them. Females are a special creation of God, and humanity would not be complete in reflecting God's greatness without them.

As you noticed from this section heading, I resurrected a has-been word to communicate something of the countercultural virtue at which we should be aiming when shepherding our boys. Okay, this medieval word may not be the bullseye, but it does point us in the right direction. The gallantry, bravery, and graciousness of the knight of another era who, at least in the caricature, would dismount his horse to assist a lady crossing a stream, gives us something of the picture of the concern and sacrifice men should make to honor women. I know that in the reverberating wake of feminism there are swaths of society that see this heightened politeness and graciousness toward women as offensive. Oh well. Writing from the "Left Coast" I do encounter that offense from time to time. Yet, even in uber-liberal California, I find that most of my efforts to show a special concern for "ladies first," opening doors for a woman, or offering to help a lady with a heavy item at the shopping warehouse is met with sincere appreciation. Either way, the special thoughtfulness, grace, and civility men ought to show toward women in general and toward their wives in particular, needs to be modeled and taught to our sons. This honors God, but it is just the beginning.

It is one thing to be polite; it is another to teach our boys to work at true kindness and understanding toward the opposite sex. Like teaching a child to parrot the words "thank you," we want to see these external expressions as a sign of the gratitude being cultivated in their hearts. Young men need to learn to appreciate the value of the very different way of thinking in young women. This does not mean we teach our boys that girls are always right, nor that girls should always have their way. It does mean, however, that our boys should not be quick to dismiss every distinctive point of view that emerges from their complementary creatures called girls. If your son is blessed to have a sister, he has a built-in laboratory, and you should capitalize on the learning opportunities this mix of perspectives provides. With that said, remember that our fallen modern culture doesn't want your boy to honor and respect females; it would have your boy cease to be distinctively male. That is sinful and altogether unacceptable. Much of the motivation to write a book about raising men is in reaction to a twisted society that would love to neuter our boys and devalue their distinctively male perspective. That must not happen.

CHOOSING A WIFE

Making graciousness and courtesy toward women one of the hallmarks of your son's childhood is the perfect backdrop for what should be a frequent discussion about your son as a future husband. Given the high probability that your son will be married, these regular childhood discussions about the special lady he will honor and respect above them all will not be wasted. How foolish parents are who provide little to no direction for their young sons about wisely choosing a wife because "after all, they are too young to be dating." By the time their sons are ready to date, those parents will have done a disservice to their teens who will then be hard-pressed to show prudence about the best kind of girl to partner up with in life. They'll be left to draw only from their hormones and maybe a couple of parental rules, instead of a richly supplied reservoir of wisdom about the kind of woman who makes for an excellent wife.

Those talks may feel formal and can't occur every month, but a

But What About . . .

BEYOND THE TALKS

Talking with your son both about sexuality and a future spouse can be a challenge at times. This may feel awkward and staged. What else can a parent do? Dad, purpose to make a regular practice of praising your son's mom for the virtues you hope his wife will possess. When your son hears these attributes of your wife hailed as something you prize and value, he will naturally learn that these are of utmost importance when it is his time to find a wife.

Moms, you can do the same without being self-aggrandizing. You don't even have to tie the quality to yourself. For instance, when you find yourself engaged in something you know is appreciated by your husband, or necessary for the good of your home, or just something you recognize is an advantage to the welfare of your family, tell your son you are praying that his future wife possesses that particular quality.

Talk often about his future wife while your son is young. It might be met with raised eyebrows at first, but this practice will soon become commonplace for him. These positive references to good and godly attributes will incrementally fill his heart with a supply of insight that will shape his idea of attractiveness, elevating his standards above the external good looks of the first girl who flips her hair and bats her eyelashes at him.

father can indirectly show him the traits to admire in a woman by his comments. Similarly, a mom can show her sons the traits she admires in a man and sees in her husband. See "Beyond the Talks" sidebar for suggestions on how to do this.

DATING

Parents have to prayerfully plan to set the rules and regulations regarding this forthcoming aspect of their son's life. As I have already tried to make clear, too many Christian parents foolishly believe that there is some safeguard in pretending that their innocent and naïve little boys would never, could never, or should never take an interest in girls—at least until they are in their midtwenties. Wrong! Expect it. And at some point, depending on the resistance of your Christian sub-culture, you may even need to encourage them in the making of social engagements with the opposite sex. The goal here is to not miss the opportunity, while your son is living under your roof, to provide wise parental oversight and thoughtful direction as they begin to navigate the emotions and temptations of relating to someone in whom they are romantically interested.

Of course the Bible is clear about the importance of sexual purity. Honest discussions and practical rules about how one can avoid temptation are critical. The maturity and demonstrated self-control of your son in other areas can help you decide the age at which you will allow social engagement with a girl he likes, as well as where, and in what contexts they take place. Regardless of how mature your son may seem to be, commonsense parameters on dating must be put in place to aid his success in controlling his youthful passions. Dating in public places, enforced curfews, and regular accountability are all essential. You'll find wisdom in some of the practices of a bygone era, like having your son sit down with the father of the girl he wants to take out. Assuming that the girl is from a solid family, direct him to open himself up to her father's concerns, guidelines, and concerns about the dating of his daughter.

Involvement with your sons in these early days of dating can yield some lasting benefits. Sure, most sons are not big on opening up to Mom and Dad about their "romantic interests," but I've found that if your discussion about girls, dating, engagement, and marriage starts long before their first crush, you'll be in a much better position to have significant input as you continue your active discipleship in this important season of life.

SANCTIFIED COMMON SENSE

Here are three practical steps you can take in parenting your son to become a man who honors God in the way he interfaces with the opposite sex.

1. Model a Healthy Marriage

Of course, making your marriage a healthy model is easier said than done. Even so, work at it. Prioritize a weekly date night with your spouse. Make it simple if you must, but make it a top priority. Take time to read good books on Christian marriage. Pray daily for your marriage to be an increasingly effective billboard of Christ's loving sacrifice and of the church's loving response. Take advantage of any Christian marriage retreats your church makes available. Submit to biblical marriage counseling when your marriage hits any rough patches. By your life, show your son that marriage can honor God and can make those of us called to it much more effective for Christ, and more joyful than we could ever be without it.

2. Utilize Electronic Aids to Accountability

Pornography is so easily available to our sons. Concern yourself with the damage this can cause, and utilize the electronic tools that can help to provide fences and safeguards to minimize the ease of access. Install whatever software you need to provide accountability. Strategically limit the placement of computers and televisions and keep them in public places. Create rules about the portable devices; keep them out from behind closed doors. Promote accountability. Periodically ask very direct questions. Encourage or even set up accountability with responsible Christian accountability partners who are outside of your family. During their dating years, openly utilize applications that disclose the real-time location of your son and his date.

With all of that said, understand that no safeguards or electronic fences are bulletproof. If your son's heart is not in the fight, any aids to assist his self-control will fail. Recognize that your knowledge of his sins is always second to God's knowledge of his transgressions. Keep him mindful of the ultimate concern—God's expectations of him. As I quoted often to my boys: "The eyes of the LORD are in every place, keeping watch on the evil and the good" (Prov. 15:3).

3. Respond to Their Transgression

Unless you are raising the Messiah, your son will sin—just as you did. Maybe not in all the same ways you did, but your son will certainly fail to keep all of God's commands. Our hope and prayer is that they will sin less, but you can count on the fact that their childhood will not be sinless. You need to respond to the sins you become aware of, especially the sins related to hormonal temptations, with seriousness but not shock. As a parent, you are to impose consequences; but be sure to parlay their transgressions into opportunities for learning, and help them to see the sinfulness of their sin.

Whatever you do in response, be careful not to demoralize or exasperate your children. With so much emotion and potential shame attached to these kinds of sins, you can risk making your son think that the whole of his Christian life is over because of an encounter with lust. Prayerfully seek to keep these failures in context. Yes, sin is serious and needs to be zealously battled, but God's grace is bigger than sin, and sincere confession and earnest repentance can pick up and restore those who have stumbled. Revisit Psalm 32 and 51 for the right perspective!

LGBTQ, ETC.

You are raising your son in the wake of a new sexual revolution. Our culture's campaign for so-called gender rights and gender identity "choice" is in the headlines every day. Most boys become aware in their early teens about the acronym LGBTQ. (It's lesbian, gay, bisexual, transgender, queer.) As bad, saddening, and maddening as this all might be to us as Christians, our boys need to be taught that God is still on the throne of heaven and we don't need to freak out, or feel like freaks. Remind your sons (and daughters) of His wise and holy standards. Honoring His standards for sexuality has always been and will always be costly—both personally and socially. But God knows best. As parents, being out of step with the current or the next sexual liberty championed by the avant-garde shouldn't unsettle us.

Call us old-fashioned, throwbacks, puritanical, or repressed. No problem. We're not on the wrong side of history! Actually, we as Christians will be the only ones on the right side of history. History reaches its crescendo when the mores, ethics, morals, and all of the kingdoms of this world are replaced by the kingdom of our Lord and of His Christ; He will assuredly reign forever and ever (Rev. 11:15). God's children who fought the good fight to personally uphold His standards, both sexual and otherwise, will be vindicated and highly esteemed.

PREPARE HIM TO FACE THE WORLD

The Bible is virtually silent about Jesus' childhood. Except for the one scene Luke presents to us, which depicts His tenacious priority to please God the Father at age twelve (2:41–51), we are left only with a summary of the way the Father was preparing the Son for His earthly ministry.

While our curiosity naturally craves more details about His stages of development, a summary statement proves to be quite helpful for us as parents. And since Scripture tells us that Jesus' manner of life should be the template for His people (1 John 2:6), it is natural that we would look to this short statement to make sure we are aiming at the same things with our children.

Here's how Luke's gospel (through the Holy Spirit) describes the development of Jesus throughout His upbringing: "And Jesus increased in wisdom and in stature and in favor with God and man" (2:52).

When it comes to wisdom and favor with God, most serious Christian parents are giving energy to developing these in their kids. When it comes to physical stature, most of that is on autopilot—a few prudent plans regarding a healthy diet and getting enough exercise is about all the direction the average parent needs. The missing focus of concern in this inspired summary of the Messiah's childhood is a game plan for guiding our sons to grow in favor with people. Admittedly, this is of lesser importance than growing in favor with God, but a prayerful and biblical consideration of how to help our sons develop socially is critical as we prepare them to face their world and make a difference in it for the glory of God.

THE GOAL IS NOT POPULARITY

It is important to remember that the one who as a child was growing in favor with people was also the one who ended up hearing a crowd chant for Him to be crucified as an adult (Luke 23:21). Even in the Old Testament's anticipation of the coming Christ, He is described as "one from whom men hide their faces," "despised," "rejected," and "not esteemed" (Isa. 53:3). We certainly shouldn't assume that whatever social skills Jesus cultivated as a child were somehow forgotten as an adult. No, rather, we are left to conclude that whatever it meant to "grow in favor with people" it cannot mean that Jesus was liked by everyone, voted the most popular in his class, or known as a "people pleaser." If being universally liked was not a reality for Christ, it certainly shouldn't be the goal for our sons.

Few things can be as enslaving and exasperating for our boys than parents who consciously or inadvertently coach them to be popular. This shortsighted and sinful mistake will almost always degenerate into a lifelong "fear of man," which the Bible calls "a snare" (Prov. 29:25). We never want our sons trapped in a nervous pursuit of being liked by everyone, or even most people! In fact, as God gets a hold on their lives, their character develops, and their zeal for God's truth increases, they need to be ready to disappoint their peers, their teachers, and yes, even their parents. It is interesting to note that the only childhood story of

Jesus that has been sovereignly preserved for us in God's Word, shows us not only that Jesus was zealous for God as a preteen, but that He frustrated His parents in the process (Luke 2:48).

THE GOAL: QUALIFIED FAVOR

We want our boys to learn to develop the social skills that will lead to a growing favor with the people of this world, but with a very important caveat. It must be crystal clear to our sons that their words and actions are accountable first and foremost to God their Maker. This is the most reasonable and obvious goal for God's creatures (2 Cor. 5:9). We seek to please Him—and doubly so as those who come to trust in Christ as our Savior and Redeemer (1 Thess. 4:1). We owe Him everything. He first loved us, and our preeminent concern is to lovingly please Him (Col. 1:10). Like with Jesus, such favor may be among a minority or only at certain times. This is "qualified favor": We seek to please Him, and in so doing we may, at times, find favor among those who respect our values and actions. We ought to seek to follow the example of Jesus by growing in favor with men so long as it does not displease God. As it was so succinctly put to the Roman Christians: "If possible, so far as it depends on you, live peaceably with all" (Rom. 12:18).

That was obviously not possible for three uncompromising young Israelites in Daniel 3. Hananiah, Mishael, and Azariah (aka, Shadrach, Meshach, and Abednego) could not please their God and their new king, Nebuchadnezzar, at the same time. They were considered criminals and sentenced to death. Back in Genesis 39 another young man found that he could not please both God and his employer's wife, as she continually sought to make him compromise his sexual purity. In that situation, Joseph was also unjustly convicted as a criminal, yet he did not cash in his integrity, and his resolve was found to be pleasing to God. In Acts 4, a young Peter and John realized they could not please Jesus Christ and the Jewish Council at the same time. Their commitment to please the Lord made them outlaws who found themselves repeatedly detained, threatened, and maligned.

It should be our prayer and hope that our boys, like Christ, increasingly grow in favor with people. But it is a qualified favor. It comes with limits and conditions. There will be days when you will have to tell your son that he could smooth this over, get that credit, win this award, or earn that applause, but it will come at too high a price. Our desire should be that our children become sold out to pleasing our Lord and Savior. Parents, from the beginning, we must resolve with Joshua, "As for me and my house, we will serve the Lord" (Josh. 24:15).

THE IMPORTANCE OF PEOPLE

Being resolved to serve and please the Lord will, on an average day, result in your son pleasing others more often than the boy who has no concern for God's concerns. God loves, cares for, and provides for people—both "the evil" and "the good" (Matt. 5:45). God clearly takes a loving interest in the people He has made. He values them above anything else in all creation. While the selfish boy will always end up loving things and using people, the son who grows strong in his understanding of God and His values will learn to sincerely love people and simply use things.

Love things, use people; love people, use things. Those are the options. With God's help your son can please the Lord by putting people and their needs above his self-interests and personal desires. With the strength conditioned from a growing favor with God, a young man will find more and more opportunities to please those with whom he interacts. As the apostle Paul wrote, "We who are strong have an obligation to bear with the failings of the weak, and not to please ourselves. Let each of us please his neighbor for his good, to build him up. For Christ did not please himself" (Rom. 15:1–3).

This is no easy task. We were all entrusted with the same kind of infant, who has been so impacted by the fall of Adam that he is naturally wired to obsess over putting himself first. Yet, God is gracious. Even prior to encountering the converting work of the Holy Spirit, our young sons can learn the priority of people over things, and the good and godly importance of putting others' interests before their own. Just as we would all teach our pre-converted children to restrain their inclination to hit another child in the face when they feel like doing so, we can rightly train our pre-converted sons to purposefully do good to others even before they are internally motivated by the indwelling work of the Spirit.

Think for a moment of the common encounter with the typical toddler when he is with his parents and asked to say "hello" to an adult who walks up to his mom or dad. How often do those rambunctious boys, who would loudly run headlong into a toy store with their friends, suddenly turn into shy guys who hide behind their dad's pant leg or their mother's skirt. Part of this may be due to your child being a natural introvert. Some of it is a natural fear of strangers. But continue to guide and encourage them in those situations, and you will see them become increasingly comfortable greeting and conversing with the adults you introduce them to.

Anticipate these situations and purposefully train your young sons that people matter so much to God, and that they must fight through their personal discomfort to look the adult square in the eye, and kindly and respectfully say "hello." This might seem like such a small thing that is not worth the battle, but when we tie a simple discipline like this to the instruction about the high value God places on people, along with the way your son's effort to give a kind and respectful greeting is received as a blessing to others, he will begin to acquire something the young Jesus possessed, namely, a growing favor with people.

Find those teachable moments in everyday life to attach a biblical value to people. In chapter 2, when discussing creative ways to develop a culture of prayer in your family, I suggested to pray with your sons when you hear the sirens of emergency vehicles. When you add to everyday practices like that a short statement about the value of people and why we should care when they suffer, you are laying a foundation that aids your boy to love his neighbor as he loves himself. When you see someone being rude to someone else and you ask your son, "How do you think that made that person feel?" you are working to cultivate a concern for the burdens of others. Of course, as with most of what we've been dealing with in this book, unless you are faithful to cultivate this value of others in your own heart, you'll be hard-pressed to see it passed on to your child. We must all pause to consider the tremendous intrinsic value that exists in *every* human life, because they are all created in the image of God.

THE PERSISTENT
BATTLE WITH SELFISHNESS

Knowing your boys were born with a bent to exalt themselves and put their interests first, be sure to have a relevant conversation when they act or speak with pride. Take time to discuss what God thinks of pride and self-promotion. God couldn't have been clearer about the problem of egotism, boasting, and arrogance:

> Everyone who is arrogant in heart is an abomination to the LORD; be assured, he will not go unpunished. (Prov. 16:5)

> For everyone who exalts himself will be humbled, and he who humbles himself will be exalted. (Luke 14:11)

> God opposes the proud but gives grace to the humble. (James 4:6)

If you do not instill in your son a vigilance about the pride that can so easily permeate his entire outlook on life, then there will be no hope of him growing in favor with people. If he is not cautioned to identify and battle this perennial temptation, not only will he become a self-centered brat, but he will put himself in opposition to God.

God knows firsthand the horrific impact of a heart that fills with pride. It was the first sin in the universe. It was the breach in the heart of an angelic being that led to a cascading series of transgressions that marred all of creation. When God warns you, me, and your son about being arrogant, prideful, or self-promoting, it must come with the pain of that initial act of iniquity.

God loves us and responds to pride with displeasure. So should we. As parents, we cannot afford to look the other way when our sons display signs of pride. The self-aggrandizing words, the boastful comment, and the snobbish condescending remark—these must all be nipped when they appear. A text of Scripture that reverberated through the halls of our home when we caught these types of words sliding out is from Proverbs 27:2: "Let another praise you, and not your own mouth; a stranger, and not your own lips." We are all for passing around sincere comments of affirmation to one another, but we have always had a well-known zero-tolerance policy about those boomerang compliments and congratulations. Like the mother of the great prophet Samuel, we must consistently teach our boys to "Talk no more so very proudly, let not arrogance come from your mouth" (1 Sam. 2:3).

Parents too often see overt behavioral infractions of house rules as the stuff worthy of discipline. But what an important lesson we fail to impress upon our boys when we don't take seriously the subtle and insidious reflections of the sin that took down the universe. I am not talking about the debatable comment that may or may not come from an inflated view of oneself. I am referring to those actions or words that obviously stem from a pompous or patronizing attitude. God takes these prideful attitudes seriously, and so should we.

THE INESTIMABLE VALUE OF HUMILITY

When the Bible says that God "gives grace to the humble" (1 Peter 5:5; James 4:6), we ought to pause to consider what a huge statement that is. Not only are we talking about the general favor of God that makes such a big difference in countless lesser ways, but the kind of grace that is at the heart of the gospel.

Nothing is more important than that your son become a forgiven child of God. The human experience of true repentance from sin and genuine faith in Christ are acts made possible by God in the fertile soil of a humble heart. The humble are able to see their need, and by grace are enabled to cry out to God for His forgiveness.

Jesus put it like this: "Everyone who exalts himself will be humbled, but the one who humbles himself will be exalted" (Luke 18:14).

But What About . . .

THE POWER OF HUMILITY

A parent may ask, "Why should I ask my son, who lacks confidence, to feel humbled?" The truth is, when parents and their children become humble before God, they can have confidence that Jesus can use them and will exalt them.

In the parable of the Pharisee and tax collector who prayed in the temple, the collector knew his faults and prayed for mercy, causing Jesus to say, "This man went down to his house justified. . . . For everyone who exalts himself will be humbled, but the one who humbles himself will be exalted" (Luke 18:14).

To the young man who is humble before God and others, God will grant His grace and favor before man (Isa. 66:2).

In the parable of a Pharisee and tax collector, the tax man lowered his head before God, beat his breast, and declared, "God, be merciful to me a sinner!" (v. 13).

This is the kind of work at humbling oneself that needs to start during your son's childhood. Keeping the stakes in mind as you consider responding to the rolled eyes, the belittling attitude, or the expression of self-admiration might just bring the appropriate motivation you need to talk about the cost of pride and the value of humility.

Humility is not only an essential component of one's conversion to Christ; it is also the consistent ingredient found in those who are used by God in great ways. This rarefied group in the Bible is as diverse as one could imagine—from brilliant scholars to simple fishermen, from the lauded professional to the teenage shepherd. Yet a common trait unites them. When it comes to their self-perception, they are all truly humble men and women.

Consider Mary, the mother of Jesus, who in her exclamation of praise in response to the announcement that she would carry and nurse the Messiah, was quick to laud the Lord like this:

> He has looked on the humble estate of his servant. For behold, from now on all generations will call me blessed; for he who is mighty has done great things for me, and holy is his name. And his mercy is for those who fear him from generation to generation. He has shown strength with his arm; he has scattered the proud in the thoughts of their hearts; he has brought down the mighty from their thrones and exalted those of humble estate. (Luke 1:48–52)

Reflecting the humble psalm of Hannah (back in 1 Samuel 2), Mary knew that God gives grace to the humble by enlisting them to important roles in His work. I'm sure she could have guessed that it wasn't the "rich young ruler" of Matthew 19 who would find a prominent place in the inner circle of Christ's ministry, but that it would be the "last" like Peter, James, Matthew, and John. As Jesus said when the prideful ruler turned and walked away, in God's economy it is always true that the world's "first" end up "last" and the world's "last" are promoted to be "first" in the work of God.

All of this should come as no surprise to the one who is thoroughly acquainted with the Bible. God has frequently and consistently promised that "this is the one to whom I will look: he who is humble and contrite in spirit and trembles at my word" (Isa. 66:2). If you rightly aspire for your son to be a man who makes a difference for God in this world, then he must continue to grow in favor with people; this cannot happen without the kind of grace that God promises to grant to the young man who is humble.

THE EXPRESSION OF
LOVE AND HUMILITY: SERVICE

The social development of our boys from a biblical perspective requires the cultivation of love for others and a right perspective of themselves. The expression of that love with humility is service. When the Bible highlights the virtue of Christ's love and humility in key passages like Philippians 2, we immediately read of His extreme efforts and costly sacrifice for us. God calls us all to reflect that paradigm. He defines that humble love by the extent of his service. Plainly put, "By this we know love, that he laid down his life for us, and we ought to lay down our lives for the brothers" (1 John 3:16).

Needless to say, it would be of no value for any one of us to "lay down our lives for the brothers" in the same manner as Christ did, by offering to be nailed to a Roman cross. John the apostle had something else in mind that we should have in mind for our sons; namely, having them learn to express their love and humility by offering to lay down their Saturday afternoon or Wednesday night to benefit others. The way to train or condition a child to willingly lay down the assets of their time and effort for the good of others, begins by parents requiring that they do so. A childhood pattern of expectation from Mom and Dad forms a habit that God uses to cultivate a love and humility within him.

"I Don't Want to Make My Son a Hypocrite!"

Again many object at this point. "I don't want to make my son a hypocrite," I hear periodically. "I will wait for his heart to stir him, so that when he serves others it is from his heart!" It is interesting that we never seem to employ this logic when it comes to personal hygiene or going to visit Grandma's house. Of course we would like for them to care (from the heart!) about clean bodies and healthy teeth, love for their grandparents, and respect for their elders. But no rational parent waits until they "feel like it," to have them brush their teeth or hug their grandpa. We set these behavioral expectations, and God consistently uses these habits to generate the motivations in our kids that keep them going. This is the essence of the promise so often quoted concerning the task of parenting: "Train up a child in the way he should go; even when he is old he will not depart from it" (Prov. 22:6).

Why does this so often happen? Not because adult children are afraid they will be grounded by their aging parents! It happens so often because the disciplined patterns of life regularly precede the internal interest in the actions. Require that your son brush and floss twice a day, and this pattern will begin in every child—I'll confess—as a form of "hypocrisy," at least to the extent that he has no sincere interest in his dental health. Yet by the time he is thirty-five he will still follow this routine. He will continue to brush and floss without his mom requiring it, because he has learned to care about the things that prompted his parents to insist on the pattern.

165

Insist on Service

So, Christian moms and dads, insist on service—Christian service, first and foremost. He needs to give of his time and effort to ministries and activities of the church as soon as those opportunities become available for kids his age. If your AWANA program has a "Leaders in Training" program, require it of your son. If your church's "Clean-up Saturday" has something a grade school boy can tackle, sign him up to be there. If there is a constructive way in your church ministry program for a young man to serve in the hospitality ministry, the retirement home-care visits, the preschoolers' summer vacation Bible school craft time, or whatever might find his help helpful, get him signed up and involved. Throughout his childhood, service to others should be non-optional.

The Bible instructs: "As we have opportunity, let us do good to everyone, and especially to those who are of the household of faith" (Gal. 6:10). The people of God are first and foremost, but we ought to keep our eyes open for ways to enlist our boys in serving the community as well. In some churches there are plenty of opportunities for community service built into the programming structure of their ministries. And yet, many of these ministries can't reasonably provide constructive avenues of service for a six-year-old boy or a twelve-year-old young man. If not, look for ways to make these happen as you read of needs at their school or see service endeavors in your community.

It can be as easy as asking for a list of church members who are in local nursing homes or elder care facilities. I remember one Christmas day deciding to take our boys with my wife and me to make the rounds to visit these shut-ins, while most of my boys' peers were busy enjoying their newly unwrapped toys. What an impact it made as we brought cookies and flowers to our shut-in members, and then proceeded down the hallways to greet and visit with complete strangers. Service outings like these make a lasting impression and build habits of service and sacrifice that help our sons to get their eyes off of themselves, and onto a world of people who need their love and attention.

SANCTIFIED COMMON SENSE

Again, allow me to wrap this up by practical ways our boys can follow Christ's example of growing in favor with the people who populate their lives.

1. Hygiene and Grooming

The world's take on personal hygiene and grooming is most often prioritized out of concern for oneself. But as boys seek to honor Christ, smelling good and looking presentable should not be for the sake of self-promotion or to impress people but out of respect for others. The goal is not "dressing for success" or "making sure my breath doesn't stink so people won't think I'm a loser." Instead, let's challenge our boys to take some interest in their appearance and be cautious about their ever evolving odors for the benefit of the people around them.

It is never about pushing the envelope with our clothing, haircuts, or fashion to express his "individuality," to make a statement, or to get attention, but rather to show that he has a genuine concern about the individuals he comes in contact with every day. What is appropriate, acceptable, and respectful? These are the questions that can keep mints in their pockets and a little gel in their hair.

2. Respect for Authority

Whether it be teachers, coaches, pastors, or small-group leaders, teach your son the importance of expressing sincere esteem for the people placed in authority. God doesn't give us or our sons permission to be disrespectful or insolent toward leaders, simply because they are bad ones. Consider the command from Peter when the malicious and immoral despot Nero was ruling over the Roman Empire: "Honor everyone. Love the brotherhood. Fear God. Honor the emperor" (1 Peter 2:17). When Paul started insulting his accuser, and then was told his accuser was the ruling high priest, he apologized and said, "I did not know, brothers, that he was the high priest, for it is written, 'You shall not speak evil of a ruler of your people'" (Acts 23:5). Let us follow the God-breathed parental instruction found in Proverbs that appeals: "My son, fear the LORD and the king, and do not join with those who do otherwise" (24:21). Honoring words, respectful attitudes, notes of gratitude, and restraint from disparagement will go a long way, especially in our day, toward godly growth in favor with people.

3. Gratitude and Thank-You Notes

Concerning those notes of gratitude, a simple habit of your son learning to genuinely express thanks to those who bring advantage to his life, will make him a standout in a world of ingrates. The Bible predicted that as the present age continued toward the end, the world's cultures would be increasingly known for their ingratitude (2 Tim. 3:2). Require of your boy, as early in his life as possible, to say thank you to waiters, bus drivers, Sunday school teachers, schoolmates, and anyone else who does something for them. Insist that they write timely thank-you notes, which are sent out for every gift they receive at Christmas, birthday, or on any other occasion.

Even before they can write, have them dictate to you their simple yet thoughtful words of gratitude as *you* write the note: "This is what Johnny said to me about your gift...." Train your son to bring a note, and even a small gift, at the end of the school year to his teacher, AWANA leader, and Sunday school teacher. Teaching this forgotten art is sure to aid your child in growing in favor in the eyes of his generation.

4. Learning to Converse

As mentioned earlier, young boys are naturally quick to hide behind the skirt of their mother when asked to say hello to someone at the supermarket or in the lobby of the church. Requiring that they learn to come out from behind your leg to make eye contact and greet the family friend is a great first step. Beyond teaching respectful greetings at a young age, there ought to be the strategic training of how to carry on conversations at various events, gatherings, and dinners. Remind them of the timeless, yet neglected exhortation to "be quick to hear, slow to speak" (James 1:19). While this is not a license or an encouragement to clam up and not speak when people are around, it is certainly an essential prerequisite to being enabled to speak wisely. Notice the blessing to those who receive wise words: "To make an apt answer is a joy to a man, and a word in season, how good it is!" (Prov. 15:23).

As previously recommended, pray with your son on the way to any event involving potential conversation, and ask God to give him ears to really hear those who speak to him. Pray that God would give him words that would benefit the hearer. May it be said of our sons that they are living examples of the standard set forth in God's Word: "Let no corrupting talk come out of your mouths, but only such as is good for building up, as fits the occasion, that it may give grace to those who hear" (Eph. 4:29).

5. Giving Apologies

Of course, there will be times when your son's words or actions cause genuine damage and hurt. This is unavoidable. What is important when this happens is that he has learned to offer heartfelt apologies. The "I'm sorry *if* I offended you" won't cut it for Christians. Our biblical standard is confession (James 5:16). When we sin against others we must "confess" the wrong we have done. "Confess" in James 5:16 comes from a vivid Greek word made up of "the same" and "to speak." In other words, we must learn to "say the same thing" about our transgression as the offended party would say.

Of course we do not teach our boys to lie about a wrong they did not commit, but when they do wrong to someone they must offer an earnest agreement that what they did or said was incorrect, inappropriate, and just plain old wrong. Learning to do this without employing excuses or rationalizations will be welcomed as a refreshing trait in a day when few people take responsibility for any of their misdeeds.

6. *Praying and Prayer Lists*

A key way of growing in favor with others—a Christlike goal—is by having a growing prayer list. When we pray for others we learn to care for others. When we spend more than a couple of seconds throwing up a name before God, but instead learn to truly intercede for the good of those on our prayer lists, our hearts will invariably be motivated to selflessly do them good when we exit the prayer closet. The best direction I can give you to see your son cultivate the godly favor of those with whom he interacts is to teach him to pray for others.

Make a prayer list for him that includes the names of his friends, classmates, teachers, coaches, the school principal, and even a few acquaintances he just met. Pray with him through that list at the kitchen table before the day gets started and at the end of the day as you tuck him in bed. Send him into a quiet corner of the house to pray through a couple of names on his prayer list before he starts his homework or before you leave to go to church.

These times of asking for God's favor and blessing in the lives of those he connects with on a daily basis will positively influence his conversations and his actions toward those people. Not only will this increase his favor with others, a strengthened prayer life will also lead him to growing in favor with God.

A RIGHTEOUS MAN'S FUN AND GAMES

Allow me to paint you a chilling picture of a thirty-two-year-old unmarried "boy" sitting in the basement of his parents' house. He works part time at a fast food dive, sleeps in late, and likes to watch ESPN when he's not at work. Typically he plays video games all night long, ordering pizza at midnight. He invites his pals over to play poker on the weekends.

Not the image of a son most parents would cherish. Yet the number of these grown-up "boys" is increasing by the year.[1] You can do something to help prevent your son from later joining these ranks of at-home "players."[2] You should. You must.

Much of what has come before in this book can help to steer him away from becoming a perpetual adolescent who lives in your basement (or his former bedroom, now reclaimed). Yet the natural lure of playing games, having fun, and chillin' out is so strong in males that unless we help our boys find the proper role of "fun and games" in the life of a godly man, he might just boomerang his way back home.

LAUGHTER, A GIFT OF GOD

Unless you find a perverse pleasure in being austere and glum, I'm sure you thankfully recognize the value of our God-given capacity for fun and laughter. Though we can't point to passages of Jesus playing games or telling jokes with His disciples, it would be hard to imagine that the perfect Man, even as serious as His redemptive mission was, did not have periodic experiences of levity and laughter with His friends. We certainly see His wit and the comedic hyperbole in several of His parables.

We also can read biographical writings of godly men who knew how to have fun. Consider Charles Spurgeon. Though Spurgeon was a serious preacher proclaiming a serious message, William Williams knew him well enough to be able to later reflect:

> What a bubbling fountain of humor Mr. Spurgeon had! I laughed more, I . . . believe, when in his company than during all the rest of my life besides. He had the most fascinating gift of laughter I ever knew in any man and he had also the greatest ability for making all who heard him laugh with him. When someone blamed him for saying humorous things in his sermons, he said, "He would not blame me if he only knew how many of them I keep back."[3]

I'm not claiming that Jesus or preachers were jokesters, but we should admit that godliness is certainly not incompatible with fun and lightheartedness. As parents, we should not be aiming to eliminate the enjoyment of chuckling and amusement from our boys' lives. Just writing that sentence reminds me that I have met very few people in our generation who need that reminder. But just in case you do—there you go.

IT'S EASY TO OVERDO IT

Most parents today, without giving it much thought, are all too quick to supply their children one comedic and amusing experience after the next. Because they take such joy in seeing their children laugh and express their happiness, the unspoken goal for many modern moms and dads has become to provide them with a steady stream of zany videos, funny stories, jokes, games, rides, and trips to the arcade or amusement park. Before you accuse *me* of being austere and glum, just take a minute to get our modern child-raising experience in perspective. You don't have to be a historian to realize that today's generation of young boys are enmeshed in an environment of fun and games that your grandfather or great-grandfather knew nothing of. The growing number of boys stuck in perpetual adolescence certainly has something to do with the programming of their youth.

Many have begun to observe the counterproductive effect we are having on our children when we saturate their childhood with toys and games.[4] At the outset of our parenting we must consider that granting the boys we love all the entertainment, amusement, fun, and games their little hearts desire is in fact something less than a loving provision. If they learn early on to be content only when they are in the midst of a fun-filled activity, a thrilling pursuit, or an entertaining performance, their childhood appetites might become their midthirties demands.

Our games and play should be social and interactive (see "But What About"). Of course, there can be fun and even loud laughter at times. Again, I have to be clear; I am not recommending that the image of God, which should be reflected as accurately as possible in His people, ought to be devoid of levity and laughter. Yet fun and games, amusement, and entertainment are at best the garnish of a godly life and not the main dish. With that said, let us consider our boys and a wise approach to their childhood pastimes.

A PLAYFUL SEASON OF CHILDHOOD

Play is certainly one very appropriate means to any child's development and learning. By "play" I am referring to those activities our kids find fun, amusing, and enjoyable, that are largely unstructured and seemingly unproductive. In admitting they are a part of our sons' development and learning, this playful aspect of childhood proves to be productive for our boys. Games and fun activities that engage the

But What About . . .

EXCESS ENTERTAINMENT

So what's wrong with fun, games, and watching TV? Nothing, as long as it is not excessive or passive, leaving our sons' social interactions behind. TV (and YouTube) viewing in excess has produced many so-called "couch potatoes" who not only get out of shape but sit or lay alone in their house.

The late Neil Postman recognized this and so much more as depicted in his classic work, which thoughtfully analyzed the broad and lasting effects of the "television revolution" in our culture. The title of Postman's book said a lot in just four words: *Amusing Ourselves to Death* (Penguin, 1985).

Even before Postman, thoughtful Christian leaders like A. W. Tozer lamented the way the Christian family is so quick to follow the descent of the world into its addiction to frivolity—seeking to find humor in any and everything: "We laugh at things which are not funny; we find pleasure in acts which are beneath our human dignity; and we rejoice in objects which should have no place in our affections."[5]

mind, retain your child's focus, exercise his imagination, and work his body (as we considered in chapter 5) are gifts from God that assist in His purpose of shaping your son.

Play is great, but like anything in our fallen world, there must be parameters and limits set to help us avoid any kind of playful activity that does not bring glory to God. We cannot expect to honor our Creator by allowing our family members to express or positively respond to behaviors, thoughts, values, or words that violate His eternal commands.

In the very early years, this kind of filtering should prove to be less of a challenge. Rubber ducks, teddy bears, plastic keys to chew on, and the glow-in-the-dark mobile that hangs over the crib are innocuous enough, yet for me there were times I chose to diplomatically tuck away gifts and baby clothes we received for our boys that displayed insignias or cultural statements, which I wouldn't want to have to explain to my sons when they later looked back on their baby pictures. The genre of trinkets and clothes with the throwback hippie references, or the university shirts that represented institutions that are bastions of anti-God philosophy were often too much for me. That may seem extreme to some readers, but the more I had learned over the years about some of these movements or leaders from these academic circles, the more my conscience would be pushed over the edge (Rom. 14:23).

As our boys grow, so do their toy and game options. The tricycles, building blocks, dump trucks, balls, scooters, and skates are, again, innocent enough, and actually prove to be helpful instruments in the development of our sons' bodies and minds. The most common concern for parents of toddlers and elementary age boys have to do with *screen time, toy guns,* and *war motif games*—these I will address below. My general exhortation to Christian parents, as they sort through the myriad of game and toy options, is to consider how your son's heart and mind will be occupied as he engages in the activity. What effect does this interest have on him? Is it negative? Would you have any reservation if the most godly person you know walked in and saw you letting your son play that game, sing that song, laugh at those jokes, or mimic that behavior? Of course you'll never have to answer to the most godly person in your circle of friends, but it does help us to visualize the very real appointment we will have when the Holy One appears.

Let me leave you with this general consideration by quoting two passages that often come to mind when buying and participating in the recreational and entertaining options available to us in this world, whether it concerns my sons or myself:

> You must no longer walk as the Gentiles do, in the futility of their minds. They are darkened in their understanding, alienated from the life of God because of the ignorance that is in them, due to their hardness of heart. They have become callous and have given themselves up to sensuality, greedy to practice every kind of impurity. But that is not the way you learned Christ!—assuming that you have heard about him and were taught in him, as the truth is in Jesus, to put off your old self, which belongs to your former manner of life and is corrupt through deceitful desires, and to be renewed in the spirit of your minds, and to put on the new self, created after the likeness of God in true righteousness and holiness. (Eph. 4:17–24)

> And now, little children, abide in him, so that when he appears we may have confidence and not shrink from him in shame at his coming. (1 John 2:28)

GOD'S MILITARY MOTIFS

From the time our boys are toddlers, they are not only adept at grunting, growling, and erupting with explosive little male voices, but they also seem to be naturally inclined to fighting, wrestling, and mimicking anything that smacks of warfare. Many Christian parents are concerned that these "natural" inclinations are akin to the natural tendencies we should trace back to mankind's sinful fallenness.

I would be quick to agree that mankind's fall into sin has given rise to wars, conflicts, fighting, and savage criminal acts. That's why we look forward to Jesus' return to put away sin in this world. He will bring the lasting peace that the Scripture has promised, and there will be no need for war or implements of war. The prophet declares, "He shall judge between the nations, and shall decide disputes for many peoples; and they shall beat their swords into plowshares, and their spears into pruning hooks; nation shall not lift up sword against nation, neither shall they learn war anymore" (Isa. 2:4).

That will be a good day. Yet, in the meantime, as Jesus said, "You will hear of wars and rumors of wars" (Matt. 24:6). As such, until He returns, there will need to be those who step up to fight for the protection and defense of what is good and right. It will be required that warriors be trained for the security of the innocent and for the retribution of the guilty. This is God's design for human government as explained to us in the New Testament (see Rom. 13:3–4).

King David, the one God said was a man after His own heart (1 Sam. 13:14; Acts 13:22), attributed his military skills to the Lord and declared in praise that God had trained his hands for war and his fingers for battle (Ps. 144:1). There was no dismissal of war or warriors as ungodly or immoral. In the Bible, when we read of soldiers coming to inquire of Christ, John the Baptist, or the apostles, we encounter plenty of instruction about repentance and subsequent righteous living, but we do not read of any calls for them to step down from their role as warriors. In fact, John the apostle instructs soldiers "to be content with your wages" (Luke 3:14). Consider also the lyrics of the first worship song inscribed in the Bible, which lauds that "The LORD is a man of war" (Ex. 15:3). This "song of Moses" is reprised at the end of the Bible, just before Christ "makes war" at His arrival (Rev. 19:11).

This doesn't mean that war is "cool" or "desirable," but it does remind us that in this fallen world it will be necessary. Not only will it be necessary in a literal sense for soldiers, marines, sailors, and aviators, but in the Scripture, spiritual warfare is also presented as normative for every Christian. We are told to

> Put on the whole armor of God, that you may be able to stand against the schemes of the devil. For we do not wrestle against flesh and blood, but against the rulers, against the authorities, against the cosmic powers over this present darkness, against the spiritual forces of evil in the heavenly places. Therefore take up the whole armor of God, that you may be able to withstand in the evil day, and having done all, to stand firm. (Eph. 6:11–13)

The apostle Paul said he "fought the good fight" (2 Tim. 4:7), and that if we are going to "take hold of eternal life," we will need to "fight the good fight of faith" (1 Tim. 6:12). We are told that the Christian life requires an engagement in an ongoing conflict (Phil. 1:30). Suffering in the Christian life, as well as ministry, is said to be done as "a good solider" with a view to pleasing "the one who enlisted" us in this battle (2 Tim. 2:3–4). We are said to have metaphorical "weapons of our warfare" (2 Cor. 10:3–4), and that we ought to be stocked up with these "weapons of righteousness for the right hand and for the left" (2 Cor. 6:7). I could go on.

My point here is to say that a "battle-ready" mindset for a grown-up Christian life is not the same as young boys engaging in warfare play. Obviously, there should be reasonable limits placed on how and to what extent this is done. But I would contend that even if your son never goes on to serve the cause of what is right in a just war or in literal combat as a part of our armed services, there is something useful and appropriate gleaned from playing the kinds of combative games that boys are so prone to want to play.

Every parent will have to decide before God and their conscience whether they allow their sons to play with toy guns, bows and arrows, tanks, and army men. I believe it can serve a helpful spiritual purpose and in some cases a practical one. Those parents who refuse to allow it may have good reasons for giving such a prohibition to their boys, but I don't think any convincing arguments from Scripture can be included among them.

SCREEN TIME

The world your boy is growing up in is full of screens that are more than capable of capturing and maintaining his attention—not just for a few hours, but for years, and even decades. Those mobile smartphones let them scan websites, interact with friends on various social media, and watch tons of fun—and sometimes disturbing—videos from YouTube and the like.

Most twenty-first century parents intuitively realize that the effects on a kid staring at a screen for the majority of his childhood cannot be good. For the thoughtless parents who have gambled away their child's formative years with a screen-saturated diet, the results have been bad, to put it mildly. I've seen the payoff. It can be ugly. I have met with parents whose sons will not leave their rooms, refusing to come out, except for a short trip to the restroom, and some who demand food be brought to them three or four times a day. I have talked to some whose boys have been so engrossed in their smartphones, video games, and tablets/computers that they end up not showering for days and days on end.

The trends are not good. Some report that this upcoming generation spends less time outdoors than prison inmates.[6] Expectedly, it is reported that today's kids would rather play video games, watch television, or text each other than go outside. One study reported in the London *Daily Mail* found that they'd rather do just about anything than play outside—even do their homework.[7] In chapter 5 we noted the need to get our sons outside running, jumping, sweating, and playing sports; now let's consider the need to limit his screen time. It won't be easy, but your determined effort is essential in order to enforce constraints on how much time he engages in watching TV, playing video games, or messing with a smartphone or a tablet.

Carlynn and I chose not to outlaw screens altogether, to ban game consoles, or refuse to let them play with apps on Grandma's tablet. Our strategy was to make these options rare, and to insist on so many other activities and endeavors in their young lives that little time remained for them to plop down and "zone out" in front of a screen. We waited longer than most parents to let them have a video game console, and when they got one, we were very selective about the few games we were willing to let them have.

VIDEO GAMES

When our boys received their first game console and started to get games as birthday presents from friends and extended family, I initially let them have genres of games I later regretted. Naturally, I never let them play or keep a game that was rated to contain "intense violence, blood, gore, sexual content, or strong language"—just as our family (including Mom and Dad) were not going to watch a movie that was similarly rated. But as I should have known, a rating on a video game cover doesn't always tell the whole story.

Believing what I said earlier about war motifs, I originally allowed my boys to have a few different types of war, battle, and fighting games. By the time I sat down to watch them play these games, I saw that some of them contained what I would expect—jets flying sorties, commanders mobilizing a defensive strategy, and gunslingers in the streets of the Old

West. Unfortunately, I quickly discovered that others of these games were gratuitous in their depictions, unjust in their tactics, and encouraged genuine abuse in the ways a player could go about raking up points. I realized the need to vet each and every one of the games they received. Once I did my homework, I concluded that only a few had any redeeming value. The rest were tossed. This new virtual world of warfare was light-years from playing Battleship, Stratego, or Risk back in the day. At one point I finally banned the whole genre for our home.

Growing up in Southern California, our boys inevitably acquired skateboarding, snowboarding, and a variety of other "cool guy" lifestyle games. Some were fine, but again, a few games had to be tossed for being over the top in their rebellion, ghoulishness, gore, or gratuitousness. If you asked my grown boys what kind of video games their parents let them play, they would likely say, "Professional sports games." There were a few exceptions, but for the most part they would be right. Golf, baseball, football, basketball, and soccer was the standard fare for them, but even that in moderation!

Creatively crafted and beautifully designed video games can hook your boys. You may think, "As long as it is not vulgar, intensely violent, or filled with gore, so what?" Yes, there are some skills and adeptness your boy may acquire from mastering a video game, but there is so much more to their childhood than sitting mesmerized engaged in a virtual (simulated and passive) baseball season. Set ground rules early if you choose to allow this form of game playing. Church first, ministry to others before play, homework before any screen comes on, and faithfully kept bedtimes are always the decree. I should also add, keep these screens in an easily visible, high traffic, doors open area of the house, so you can monitor both the kinds of games and the time spent on them.

I would also advise you to consistently and strongly remind your son, as he sits for his designated time to play these types of games, that this is the fleeting season for such things. Sure, in our home Dad would join them occasionally to try to beat them on a few holes of their PGA video game, but as they will testify, I was incessant about telling them that the reason they should always beat their dad at such things is because games are for kids. I would often smirk and tell them, "Enjoy it now, boys. God has made you for much more important things than playing games!" I trust you can set a good example in this regard. Yes, you might have people over from time to time to play a board game or maybe even a game on a screen, but grown-up life was surely not designed by God for perpetual game-playing. Our boys need to know this.

SEEMINGLY UNCOMMON
SANCTIFIED COMMON SENSE

Again, let's conclude this topic with a few practical tidbits that may play a role in raising up a righteous man who lives a productive life and understands the proper role of fun and games in his life.

Stop Saying, "All I Want Is for My Kids to Be Happy"

For a sermon I would soon preach, I decided to chronicle some firsthand research on a passage that called us to examine what our ultimate goals are and should be. I took a cameraman and a microphone and went out into a local gathering place to interview people to discover what their life goals are. It was as though they were all reading off the same script. It seemed every other person declared that the happiness of their children was their ultimate goal—their "happiness"!

As I stated in chapter 1, I hope that line will not be the response from parents who want to raise godly men. This cultural mantra not only has no place in the hearts or mouths of parents who want to see their children grow in God's truth and become fruitful in loving and serving Christ, but when our children hear us say such things, they take note. If your boy thinks the appropriate goal for his life is "being happy," he will settle in to make choices for years and perhaps the entirety of his life based on what is fun, entertaining, enjoyable, or pleasurable for him. Remember his purpose should be to engage in what is "good and right and true" and daily seeking "to discern what is pleasing to the Lord" (Eph. 5:9–10).

Say "Yes" with Enforced Sacrifices

Adult life is filled with choices that have sacrifices attached. Our sons need to learn this early as they begin to manage and curtail their wants and desires. Too many parents give their children carte blanche, repeatedly saying "yes" to their simple requests, because the actual price tag to the parent is so small. "Why not?" the parent reasons. "It makes my son happy."

There was a phase when my young boys loved collecting sticks. Later their affections were drawn to rock collecting. I think our house would have been overrun with their neighborhood finds had my wise wife not taught them a valuable lesson early on. When the shelf next to their bed had six rocks or the floorboard of the car had six sticks, she would tell my son with the "seventh" in hand that he was welcome to satisfy his desire with that fantastic new find, but one in the collection had to go. Wow, you'd immediately see the eyebrow wrinkle and the wheels of his little brain start to grind. Here was a simple but wise way for him to count the costs and to manage and curtail his desires for satisfaction even before the object cost a thing. This lesson can be learned over and over again when it comes to toy cars, teddy bears, or anything else your child is collecting.

Permit Segments of Fun Amid Responsibility

Consider the many situations that require your young son to engage in less-than-pleasurable activities. For little boys with a perennial craving for fun and games it might be the need for them to sit quietly without fidgeting at a restaurant, while you and your spouse chat with another couple. Maybe it is bath time, or nap time, or homework time. All of these can be designed with a limited segment of fun, designed to help him burn off that pent up energy so that when it is time for work, focus, or being quiet, he is apt to succeed. At bath time, you need cooperation to get through this important necessity. You want to get through it as quickly as possible. Even so, designate a short amount of time (with that egg timer we talked about in chapter 6) for him to do nothing but play and splash around. When the time's up, it's time to get to business. No fussing or fidgeting.

My favorite restaurant has an adjacent patch of grass that my boys knew they had the freedom to go and run once they got the wink from Mom or Dad and they had politely excused themselves from the table. Meal time was their time to be quiet, eat, and color on their placemats, but their "fun time" was coming. They knew it, and it helped them. Likewise, when they were younger, their nap time started with a measured few minutes to sing, play, or talk, but when the egg timer went off, they were off to the business of napping.

Make Monday (or Another Day) Fun Day

Designated days or afternoons can serve the same weekly function the timed "segments of fun" served when your boy is little. With my schedule as a pastor, Monday had to be our "fun day" afternoon. It was adhered to like clockwork! They knew it was coming—every week. As elementary-aged boys, if Wednesday or Thursday afternoon seemed like "such a drag," filled with nothing but "work, work, work!" they could always count on something fun for that soon-to-arrive Monday afternoon. This simple principle works for kids and grown-ups. When we schedule our recreation or leisure time first and are faithful to keep it, we can more easily find the discipline and perseverance to plug away during our work time.

Give them something to look forward to. It can be an enjoyable vacation, date night, or fun day on the schedule. It may seem surprising, but those who seem to be "playing all the time" or taking too many breaks, can be far less productive than those who anticipate such welcome breaks. Segment "fun times" for your boys during the day, during the week, and during the year. This will serve to keep their (and your) appetite for fun appropriately fed, and the focus on work and responsibility where it ought to be.

Include Fun with a Purpose

Whether it is an upcoming vacation or quick trip to Grandma's house, it is wise to construct some of your fun time as something that pays dividends in other areas of your boy's life. Make your vacations about fun, of course, but also utilize part of these times to build and shape your son's worldview for Christ's sake. Don't turn the whole of your vacation into an educational field trip, but do give some thought and plan to seeing how you might make a part of that fishing trip, mountain getaway, or that East Coast excursion something that informs, warns, or instructs your son for his future. Some parents are naturals at this. Some take it too far. But for those who haven't given it much thought, do so.

You can utilize even a forty-minute freeway drive, as it was to my boys' Grandma's house. Instead of just putting on music or a video in your family van, keep a fun Bible trivia book in the glove box for commutes. Turn the drive time into a fun family game, where the youngest gets the easiest questions and Mom has to answer from the "expert" category. Have fun and let these laugh-filled competitive games springboard into short discussions about the lessons from the Bible stories or facts you come across.

Training and directing our boys toward a godly manhood does not need to quash the joy or fun of childhood. It doesn't need to extract one's sense of humor or their ability to laugh and periodically make a joke. After all, godly men know the joy and fulfillment of living at peace with their Maker. Our hope and prayer for our boys is that they learn to manage their fondness for fun and games, finding its proper role in their lives without it taking over. May our prayerful parenting guide them in their recreational choices and allow them to find the righteous boundaries God would want them to maintain as they live productive lives for Him in this world.

WISDOM TO NAVIGATE THE TEEN YEARS

There's one word that stirs up plenty of emotions in parents: *teenagers*. Because every parent has been one, there is good reason for such a visceral reaction. Some modern "authorities" insist that the very concept of an adolescent is an unnecessary social construct, yet there is no doubt changes abound during the teen years.

The emotional, physiological, and spiritual transitions that will take place in your son during the teen years will present you with some unique challenges—unlike any other period in his life.[1]

I'm sure you can think back to your own teenage years and recall the unparalleled experience of passions, conflicts, discoveries, outbursts, and reactions which were undeniably tied to the many changes your body was going through. As thoughtful Christian parents, we need to get ready to manage our sons during these turbulent years. We need to wisely think through how to coach our young men into their fast-approaching adult life. We have already referred to the teen years when it comes to such issues as curfew, time management, and his growing sexual awareness, but raising men from boys during their adolescent years requires special attention. Therefore, this final chapter.

While we cannot deny a number of effects from the biological turmoil of this transitional period, let us never use the label as an excuse to "let teen boys be teen boys." I have encountered far too many parents of wild and rebellious teens who simply shrug their shoulders and dejectedly say, "He's a teenager. . . . Whatcha gonna do?" This won't fly for those parents making a claim to godliness. Consider the parenting standard for Christian leaders in the pages of God's Word. The Bible does not carve out a special exemption if their son is a "teenager." God requires that the leader's children not be "open to the charge of debauchery or insubordination" (Titus 1:6). The high standard the Lord lays out cannot be set aside because a parent wants to excuse his son as a "crazy" adolescent.

INDEPENDENCE AND POWER STRUGGLES

Throughout the middle school and high school years, even a well-taught and well-mannered son can be expected to want, ask, or even demand increasing freedoms and independence from your oversight, rules, and restrictions. This transitional stage of life is marked by young men who believe they are capable in many ways of taking care of their own daily business without your "interference." Of course, they have little—and in some cases—no appreciation for mortgage payments, electricity bills, insurance premiums, house maintenance and repairs, and the list goes on. They innately feel that desire for autonomy, yet without the resources or ability to be truly self-governing. We can all sympathize with the feelings of wanting to be self-reliant, but as parents we have learned much about what comes with that wish.

Instead of being like many parents who simply square off with their teens in weekly power struggles, we ought to wisely begin to help them appreciate their increasing independence with a steady stream of responsibilities, which will help him see the price of being the one who calls the shots.

How do we do this? Sit down with your spouse and map out the transfer of domestic and life duties he should have from age thirteen to eighteen. Together ask, "At what age will we hand over the task of preparing his own sack lunches? At what age will we have him take over the task of washing and folding all his own clothes? At what age do we want him to fill out all the forms at the doctor's office or for the first day of school? When will he be expected to pay his own phone bill?" Planning out the teen years in this way provides your son with a proactive wake-up call to what independence requires. It won't eliminate those conflicts in which you'll hear, "I should be allowed to do that," but I have found it will mitigate the constant calls for more freedom. It will at least make him think twice.

MOMS AND SONS

The power struggles and general detachment of teenage sons are the hardest on moms. If you are a first-time mother of a teenage son or anticipate being one soon, be warned. It is painful on a number of fronts. Dads generally take pride in their sons standing on their own. Moms, on the other hand, often cry their way through those stages. The little boy who used to scurry up to hug your neck as hard as he could with that genuine look of affection and adoration, now wants you to butt out of his business. He wants privacy. He refuses your help. Add to this pain the fact that those looks of genuine affection and adoration have now fixated on a teenage girl in his calculus class he can't stop thinking about. The seeming rejection and the feelings of being edged out of your boy's heart can feel unbearable.

DADS AND SONS—AND THEIR MOMS

First, you have to strongly insist that your son treat his mother with the greatest respect. Sure, you can understand his desire to grow up and the fact that he doesn't feel like he needs "a mommy" anymore, but it is your job to make sure he goes out of his way to treat his mother with honor as the Bible clearly requires! Remember that the initial command to honor one's parents in Exodus 20:12 was given to a gathered assembly primarily made up of adults. Yes, the command includes the call for children to obey their moms and dads, and it clearly carries with it the implication of financially caring for an elderly parent, but between those two extremes, are decades of showing honor.

Dad, teach your son that any eye-rolling, raised voices, or disrespectful exchanges with his mother are not only a violation of God's command to treat His daughter (your son's mother) with respect, but this woman is also your wife! I hope every teenage son has at least one dreadfully memorable exchange with his serious father, wherein Dad insists that this smelly, hairy, lanky young man in his house treat his beloved wife with dignity and honor.

Next, you dads need to lovingly and carefully lead your wives to begin to let go. Little by little, year by year, this teenage season is a transition from dependence to independence. It is hard for us as dads too, but we had better suck it up, put on a brave face, and help our dear wives give our boys more and more of the independence they will rightly require to mature into manhood.

Doubling your investment in your marriage during these teenage years is important. So often dads of teens are just hitting their stride in their careers, and opportunities for advancement often abound. Say no to some of that if you have to, and give yourself more and more to your bride. Plan a fun trip to somewhere special. Surprise her with a fun weekend getaway for just the two of you. Take an extra date night every week. Plan more long walks and talks. Your love and support during these years of "losing her boy" is important. Even if you've had the right mindset from the beginning, going through these stages of increasing (and appropriate) separation and stepping back from your son's everyday life require more of your compassionate devotion to your wife.

In our broken world, I know divorced parents will be reading this; I can imagine that the last paragraph left you, a single parent, feeling disheartened. Don't be. Your situation may be impaired by having to navigate your son's teen years without a spouse, but I am writing this book to Christians. There shouldn't be a Christian reading this

But What About . . .

WHEN DAD'S NOT IN THE PICTURE

If you're a single parent, you may wonder how one can raise men alone. A single mother acutely feels the compounding of that challenge when it comes to the final years of parenting a teenage boy. Mom, if you are navigating this final season alone, I would insist that you draw near to your church family like never before. There are youth group leaders, pastors, deacons, ministry assistants who can be strong male leaders in your son's life.

Such important relationships may not emerge without your concentrated effort to orchestrate them, but they are more than possible. Countless young men have been discipled and coached through their teen years by godly mentors who have generously and selflessly taken the necessary time to invest their lives.

If there is no strong Christian grandfather, uncle, or older cousin in your family, boldly look to your spiritual family for assistance.

book who doesn't have a church family. That family is tremendously important. You must realize that though there is an increasing personal detachment that comes with parenting a son through his teenage years, especially his later teen years, your connection with your church, its people, and ministries can and should rightly increase.

DR. JEKYLL AND MR. HYDE?

The hormonal changes inundating your son's body and brain during his teenage years may make you wonder if you have raised the next Dr. Jekyll and Mr. Hyde. During these years, mood swings are to be expected. You likely had them too. Your son might be seriously bummed out in the morning, over-the-top euphoric in the afternoon, and intensely angry by the time dinner is over. It happens. Your goal is to help him exercise a level of self-control that can keep him from speaking, deciding, and texting when his emotions are swinging high or low. One of the most repeated exhortations to our teenage sons during these years was to "pray about it, and sleep on it." Remember the prophet Elijah, after his mountaintop experience of defeating the prophets of Baal, which was followed immediately by the desert experience of being chased by the wicked Queen Jezebel, and despaired of life (1 Kings 19:1–4). Like Elijah, your son will find that a good night sleep, a decent meal, and a conversation with God can lead to much clearer thinking and better decisions.

We all have the mountaintop highs of a big victory and the discouragement of feeling defeated in the desert, yet our teenage sons seemingly go through that cycle once a day. So be gracious. Be sympathetic. There's no allowance for transgression. There's no justification for sinful outbursts. Yet we can show compassion and kindly understand the volatile mix of emotions and the unique pressures of that special season of life, and that should give us some perspective. Our empathy should influence how we pray for our sons and make us ready to forgive when their failures are pointed out and confessed.

JUNIOR-HIGH HUMOR

Before high school there is junior-high. Inevitably, your son and his friends will learn the kind of humor that seems to uniquely rattle the funny bone of junior-high boys. The home you raised your son in may have been untarnished from the rude and crude bathroom humor so common to adolescents, but it has a way of finding your boy. So don't be surprised when farting, belching, spitting, and anything related to bodily functions becomes the height of comedy to your boy. Our culture doesn't do much to inhibit this brand of humor. Actually, our society seems to work overtime to ensure that it is a permanent part of every man's adult life. Many of the comedy movies that do so well at the box office seem aimed at seventh-grade boys. And yet these movies and their jokes will attract and appeal to the baser part of people from almost every demographic.

While it may be impossible to imagine a junior-high boy who isn't going to laugh at someone passing gas in his classroom, I do believe we have a responsibility as parents, especially as Christian parents, not to prolong or feed this natural appetite for immature bathroom humor. I would suggest there is a whole genre of comedies that just aren't worth him or you seeing. Ever. There will be enough taking place in their own junior-high universe that provokes that sort of laughter. I certainly don't need script writers and foley artists to add to their hunger for base humor. When at home and some inevitable situation along these lines prompts a laugh from the whole family, I'd recommend saying, as I did, "That was our quota for the week." As with certain words or topics of discussion, I would often on the spot make up a quota for that subject. "That's a once a month word," or "That is enough on that topic for two weeks."

Profanity or vulgarity should never be allowed, but in the course of everyday life there will be unavoidable issues, descriptions, or comments that arise, which you'd hate to see become normal fare for your boy. An assortment of indelicate topics will surely make their peers roar with laughter, egging them on for more, but as parents we ought to raise the bar of civility and decorum even during their junior high and high school years.

In every situation, let us remain mindful of what is never appropriate for the people of God:

> But sexual immorality and all impurity or covetousness must not even be named among you, as is proper among saints. Let there be no filthiness nor foolish talk nor crude joking, which are out of place, but instead let there be thanksgiving. For you may be sure of this, that everyone who is sexually immoral or impure, or who is covetous (that is, an idolater), has no inheritance in the kingdom of Christ and God. Let no one deceive you with empty words, for because of these things the wrath of God comes upon the sons of disobedience. (Eph. 5:3–6)

We should never be willing to laugh, nor allow our children laugh, at the things that will bring judgment to the lost people of this world.

"HOW DO I LOOK?"

You may not ever hear the words "How do I look?" come out of his mouth, but you can be sure the concern is in his mind. Were this a book for teenage girls, this section would likely need multiple chapters, as friends, movies, and other media put increased pressure for our daughters to "look good." Your teenage boy also will struggle with how he looks; to refuse to acknowledge this is akin to sticking your head in the sand. The teenage years bring new and increasing concerns with appearance. Everyone likes to be liked. We all want to look good. If people were honest, they'd admit they would like to be considered attractive. All of that starts in earnest during one's teen years. To know that concern is there, especially in boys who want to pretend they don't care, is important for every parent.

As you can recall from your own teenage experience, peers are particularly cruel when it comes to anything that they do not consider attractive. And it can be argued that even attractive people are hit with a special kind of teenage disdain. With all of that going on, it is important to avoid what should be obvious. If your boy is short for his age, you must not give him added reason to feel bad about that reality. If he is tall for his age. If he is portly. If he is lanky. If he is pale. If his hair is too curly. If his hair is thin. I could go on. I know parents look at their children through a lens of parental love that makes all of those attributes endearing, but his peers don't share those spectacles. Critical comments about his appearance can be almost as devastating to a teenage boy as you would imagine them to be to a teenage girl.

Do what you can to carefully and diplomatically get all of that in perspective. Of course "the LORD sees not as man sees: man looks on the outward appearance, but the LORD looks on the heart" (1 Sam. 16:7). That we know, and it is our paramount concern as Christian parents. But stating that fact can't erase the natural concern teenagers have while in this stage of caring about whether they are attractive to the opposite sex. Within reason, help them through these challenges. If they are in their divinely scheduled acne breakout, do what you can to nonchalantly help them mitigate the effects. Without going overboard in trying to eliminate this teenage rite of passage, casually give them tips, and help with fresh pillowcases, face soaps, and acne cream.

I say "nonchalantly" and "casually" because how you go about assisting them with their face or their fitness can demoralize them or embarrass them. They can push back or retract, making things worse and closing the door to your help. Even the most intrepid son with the most courageous, strong, and unflinching personality is pretty fragile regarding his appearance during a few of his teen years. Say less. Offer help with a cool and calm demeanor. Dads, give them tips on how to dress appropriately for a variety of occasions. Teach them to shave at the right time (better too soon than too late!). Get them the gear they need for trimming their sideburns, taming their armpits, and keeping their shoes from stinking. Shop with them for a decent smelling and sparingly applied cologne. Take an interest, without seeming more concerned than they are willing to admit they are.

When they ask you to step back, I'd do so, but not completely. With the average teen, their interest in their appearance will occasionally surface with opportunities for you to be of help. It's not vain, conceited, or worldly. Supporting your teenage son as he settles into adult life as a well-groomed man is necessary.

DRUGS AND ALCOHOL

Unless you raise your boy in a plastic bubble, he will encounter opportunities during his teenage years to take drugs and drink alcohol. Even if you have your teen sequestered now in a plastic bubble, as soon as he steps out of it at eighteen or whatever year you release him from it, he will be hit with the offer of alcohol and drugs. The preparation to encounter this temptation, I trust began long before his teenage years. It should. Shielding him from the fact that drugs and alcohol are the most common tools the enemy utilizes to destroy lives is foolish. Even if your boy is five or six years old, as your life intersects with stories and situations that illustrate the devastation of these vices, you should reinforce the need to avoid these popular means of recreation.

Be sure you teach your son that legality never equals morality. God is interested in His children living righteous and godly lives. Currently the law of the land allows all sorts of activities that are immoral and unrighteous. It was no different in the days of the Bible. Our standard is God's truth, not the government's laws or the next state proposition. While, for now, states still ban alcohol and drugs for minors, all the talk of legalized marijuana, for instance, adds to one's teenage mind that there is no real harm in these things. Starting early is just jumping the gun a little. Remind them that Christians care little what the country's law allows; we live to "discern what is pleasing to the Lord" (Eph. 5:10).

It is important to teach your sons that the God of the Bible is pro-sobriety. The goal of reflecting the image of God in our human lives is to always favor being alert, clear thinking, perceptive, aware, attentive, sensible, and in control of one's faculties. Inversely, the Bible consistently sees a disconnect between human dignity and intoxication, inebriation, impairment, lethargy, being unrestrained, befuddled, or being "under the influence" of a substance, as we would say. God always condemns these traits and all sixteen examples of people being intoxicated in the Bible are presented in a bad light. Being inebriated is wrong (Eph. 5:18; Prov. 31:4–5).

Though we can't point to passages that speak at any length to the problem of drugs, we can plainly see that toying with one's body chemistry for fun is not allowed. Whether it is alcohol, marijuana, a restricted medication, or anything else, such substances should not be used to induce a physiological euphoric experience. These elements serve a purpose, but they are not to be engaged in for recreation (Eccl. 10:17). When we use them for recreation, it typically leads to various states of intoxication. Worse yet, when our body chemistry is toyed with merely to achieve the "high," the principle of diminishing returns will set us up for addiction. As a pastor on the front lines of dealing with people for decades now, I have seen the devastation of these addictions. Scripture speaks to a good purpose when we are beckoned to resolve with the apostle Paul, "I will not be dominated by anything" (1 Cor. 6:12).

It may sound like a fifth grade "red ribbon" lecture but, oh well, teach your boys to say "no" to drugs and alcohol. Not only are they illegal for minors, drugs and alcohol lead to many degrading and sinful effects. If you choose, as a parent, to exercise your freedom to drink alcohol, I would only remind you that the alcoholic beverages that are available to you today are far more potent than that wine we read of in the Bible. So be careful. Use restraint. Make sure you never cross the line and violate God's Word by being "under the influence" of a chemical.

TEENAGE ODDS AND ENDS

Let me one more time quickly address a few situations you are bound to encounter and a couple of decisions you'll be forced to make during these final years of parenting your son.

Cellphones

Your teenager will want a cellphone. Your grade-schooler will want a cellphone. If you put it off until his teenage years, you are the exception. Every parent needs to determine when and if this privilege will be granted. Most concede, at least by the time their child is a teenager. Nevertheless, having a phone should always come with provisions and conditions. These phones, as I'm sure you know, can be the source of all kinds of sin and trouble for your son. All passwords need to be known, and the phone must be accessible to Mom and Dad.

It should be agreed upon that all apps, pictures, texts, and any communication on or through the phone are available for you to see. As noted in chapter 8, your son's "privacy" is not worth risking him getting hooked on pornography, or enabling him to engage in sexting, or creating an inappropriate digital footprint that can follow him for years to come. If you suspect ungodly activity on the phone, limit when and where it can be used. If there are breaches in your standards for the use of the phone—it can always be taken away.

A Part-Time Job

Working part-time during high school can be a great introduction to the "real world" of taxes, paychecks, and dealing with bosses. I would highly recommend that you carve out a niche at some point in his high school years to land a part-time job, even if his schedule is so full that it has to be a short-term job during Christmas break or summer recess. Even so, if he can learn to be diligent, accountable, punctual, and conscientious at a place that holds a paycheck over his head, he will learn something a classroom or a parental lecture cannot teach him. You will also have an opportunity to coach him through the indispensable lessons found in key passages like this one:

> Bondservants, obey in everything those who are your earthly masters, not by way of eye-service, as people-pleasers, but with sincerity of heart, fearing the Lord. Whatever you do, work heartily, as for the Lord and not for men, knowing that from the Lord you will receive the inheritance as your reward. You are serving the Lord Christ. (Col. 3:22–24)

Ideally the job should be at school or close enough to home that he can bike or even walk to the workplace. Avoid letting him drive a car there unless he (1) is not too aggressive or too impulsive to drive safely, (2) has proven to be responsible in other areas of his life, and (3) can qualify for a driver's license. Having a license can be a good step in a young man's increasing independence.

CURFEWS

Every teenager needs a curfew. Even with all the technology that allows us to call, text, or digitally track the movements of our sons about town, a deadline to be in each night is essential. Commonsense requirements like a reasonable hour to be home on school nights, a clear plan as to where he will be and who he will be with, should always be nonnegotiable.

If your boy acquires a driver's license and proves to be trustworthy in logging a faithful record of being in on time, you might want to work toward going to bed yourself, before junior is due home. In our house, my home security system always logged the time my son arrived (which was handy). Even with that, it was hard on my wife, as I imagine it is for every mom, to follow my lead and entrust our responsible upperclassman to the Lord's care while we dozed off to sleep.

If he's a high school senior, remember it will only be a matter of months before you may be sending him off to college, and staying up to "make sure he gets home" will be an impossibility. Your son's growing independence will need to coincide with your growing confidence in God's safekeeping and oversight of his day-to-day life.

RELY ON AND CALL UPON GOD FOR HELP

No matter the obstacles or limitations, no matter how inept or under-qualified you might feel for the parenting task, whether you have every advantage in your home, or your family life is filled with liabilities, the *ultimate* success of seeing your son become a godly man depends on God. So rely on Him. If anything is clear in the Bible, it is the truth that God is the key to victory in any endeavor. Remember Solomon's wise words:

> Unless the LORD builds the house, those who build it labor in vain . . . Behold, children are a heritage from the LORD, the fruit of the womb a reward. Like arrows in the hand of a warrior are the children of one's youth. Blessed is the man who fills his quiver with them! He shall not be put to shame when he speaks with his enemies in the gate. (Ps. 127:1–5)

There are a lot of foolish and inconsequential things people are asking God to empower. But few things are more important to the Lord than the raising up of godly men (and women). Because God is the key, prayer is indispensable! Our parenting efforts must be laden and saturated by our heartfelt prayers. These prayers for the conversion, sanctification, maturity, wisdom, and fruitfulness of our children will undoubtedly rise to God as requests near and dear to His heart. Ask in faith and work in wisdom.

May God unfold before your eyes what this generation so desperately needs—another man of God.

NOTES

Introduction: A Whole New Ballgame

1. Chase Strangio, "What Is a Male Body?" July 19, 2016, http://www.slate.com/ blogs/ outward/2016/07/19/there_is_no_such_thing_as_a_male_body.html.
2. Ibid.

Chapter 1: Envision a Man's Future Every Day

1. Jonathan V. Last, *What to Expect When No One's Expecting: America's Coming Demographic Disaster* (New York: Encounter Books, 2013). Last also reports (page 2) that pets in America outnumber children "by more than four to one."
2. The call to have children is reiterated to settlers of the promised land in Deuteronomy 28:4, and even paraphrased for those exiled from the land (Jer. 29:6). See also God's words to Jacob in Genesis 35:11.
3. David M. Hoffeditz, "They Were Single Too," *DTS Magazine*, June 1, 2015; www. http://www.dts.edu/read/they-were-single-too-a-sampling-of-8-bible-characters/.
4. John Stott, "John Stott on Singleness," *Christianity Today*, August 17, 2011; http://www.christianitytoday.com/ct/2011/augustweb-only/johnstottsingle ness.html.

Chapter 2: Set His Spiritual Trajectory

1. J. C. Ryle, *The Duties of Parents* (reprint, n.p., J.C. Ryle Books, 2010), 18. Available at Amazon.com.
2. John Newton, "Amazing Grace! How Sweet the Sound," Worship and Service Hymnal (Chicago: Hope Publishing, 1957), 227.

Chapter 3: A Home That Builds Godly Men

1. Charles Murray, "Why Economics Can't Explain Our Cultural Divide," *Wall Street Journal*, March 16, 2012, https://www.wsj.com/articles/SB10001424052 70230469280457728158240339206.
2. Robert Rector, "Marriage: America's Greatest Weapon Against Poverty," (Heritage Foundation: Special Report from Domestic Policy Studies Department), No. 117, September 5, 2012.
3. For instance, avail yourself to the helpful resources at the website for The Council on Biblical Manhood and Womanhood at www.cbmw.org.
4. See James Dobson, *Bringing Up Boys* (Carol Stream, IL: Tyndale, 2001), 181–87.
5. Norman Grubb, *C. T. Studd: Cricketer and Pioneer* (Cambridge, England: Lutterworth Press, 1933; repr. Fort Washington, PA: CLC Publications, 2008), 31.

Chapter 4: Quell the Rebellion of His Sinful Heart

1. Professor Robert E. Larzelere of Oklahoma State University's Department of Human Development and Family Science reviewed several scientific studies on physical discipline; see Robert E. Larzelere, "There Is No Sound Scientific Evidence to Support Anti-Spanking Bans," April 2007, in http://humansciences.okstate.edu/facultystaff/Larzelere/nztabconts.47.pdf. Other studies are inconclusive: Carl Bialik, "New Research on Spanking Might Need a Time Out," *The Wall Street Journal*, October 14, 2009; and Laura Sanders, "The Debate over Spanking Is Short on Science, high on emotion," *ScienceNews* magazine, September 24, 2014, https://www.sciencenews.org/blog/growth-curve/debate-over-spanking-short-science-high-emotion.

2. "Welfare and Institution Code," Division 2 Children, Part 1. Article 6, "Dependent Children," sec. 6, "California Legislative Information, http://leginfo.legislature.ca.gov/faces/codes_displaySection.xhtml?lawCode=WIC&sectionNum=300.

Chapter 5: Make Him Sweat Every Day

1. Note the findings of the well-documented sociological studies found in Paul Nathanson and Katherine K. Young, *Spreading Misandry: The Teaching of Contempt for Men in Popular Culture* (Montreal: McGill-Queen's University Press, 2006) and Christina Hoff Sommers, *The War Against Boys: How Misguided Policies Are Harming Our Young Men* (New York: Simon & Schuster, 2015).

2. See James C. Dobson, "Men Are Fools" and "Boys in School" in *Bringing Up Boys: Shaping the Next Generation of Men* (Carol Stream, IL: Tyndale, 2001; repr., 2014), chaps. 12, 13.

3. "Family Christian Introduces New Protective Christian Bubble for Children," August 23, 2016, http://babylonbee.com/news/family-christian-introduces-new-protective-christian-bubble-children/.

4. Michael Ungar, "Psychologist: Stop Bubble- Wrapping Your Kids! September 17, 2014 http://www.alternet.org/culture/psychologist-stop-bubble-wrapping-your-kids-how-overprotection-leads-psychological-damage.

5. Albert Mohler, *Culture Shift* (Colorado Springs: Multnomah, 2011), chap. 10.

6. http://www.ncaa.org/about/resources/research/probability-competing-beyond-high-school.

7. Jim Reiner, "What You Need to Know about MLB Tryouts—Part 6"; http://www.ultimate-baseball-field-renovation-guide.com/mlb-tryout-what-you-need-to-know.html.

8. "Childhood Obesity Facts," Centers for Disease Control, https://www.cdc.gov/healthyschools/obesity/facts.htm.

Chapter 8: How to Raise Men in a World Half-Full of Women

1. See, for instance, Josh McDowell's *Straight Talk with Your Kids about Sex* (Eugene, OR: Harvest House, 2012). You can also consult Internet resources at Focus on the Family (http://www.focusonthefamily.com/parenting/sexuality/talking-about-sex).

Chapter 10: A Righteous Man's Fun and Games

1. For examples of young adults unemployed or underemployed with time on their hands, see Kirsten Grind, "Can You Spare a Room?", *The Wall Street Journal*, May 3, 2013; Kate Ashford, "Parents: Your College Grads Expect You to Support Them Post-College," *Forbes*, May 20, 2015; and Adam Davidson, "It's Official: The Boomerang Kids Won't Leave," *The New York Times Magazine*, June 20, 2014, at www.nytimes.com/2014/06/22/magazine/its-official-the-boomerang-kids-won't-leave.htmlwww.forbes.com/sites/kateashford/2015/05/20/post-grad-support2014.

2. Of course, many of these sons are unemployed or underemployed not for lack of trying. The market economy overall or in the field they are trained may have fewer job openings or others with better credentials for employment in a limited market. Nonetheless, there are ways we as parents can prepare them so that if they do return home for a season, they can use their time productively and not turn into bedroom or playroom vagabonds.

3. William Williams, *Charles Haddon Spurgeon: Personal Reminiscences*, rev. and ed. M. Williams (London: Religious Tract Society, 1933), 24.

4. Katy Koonz, "Taming Toy Overload," *Parenting*, n.d., at www.parenting.com/article/taming-toy-overload. See also Jonathan Leake and Tom Robbins, "Children Play Less the More Toys They Get," February 21, 2010, at http://rense.com/general8/yots.htm.

5. A. W. Tozer, comp. James L. Snyder, *Tozer on Worship and Entertainment* (Camp Hill, PA: WingSpread, 1997), 117–18.

6. Katherine Martinko, "Children Spend Less Time Outside Than Prison Inmates," March 25, 2016, www.treehugger.com/culture/children-spend-less-time-outside-prison-inmates.html.

7. Katy Winter, "Children Today Would Rather Read, Do Chores or Even Do Homework Than Play Outside," *The* [London] *Daily Mail*, April 11, 2013, www.dailymail.co.uk/female/article-2307431/Children-today-read-chores-HOMEWORK-play-outside.html.

Chapter 11: Wisdom to Navigate the Teen Years

1. Robert Epstein, *The Case against Adolescence: Rediscovering the Adult in Every Teen* (Fresno, CA: Quill Driver Books, 2007).

The love she craves,
the confidence you need

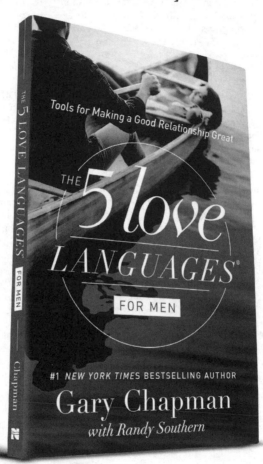

Capture teachable moments with the Scripture

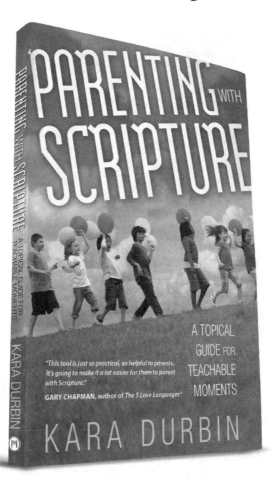

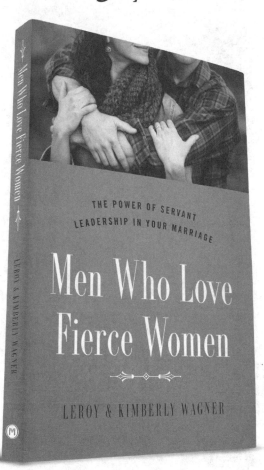